BUILT ON PRINCIPLE

A Guide to Family Foundation Stewardship

Elaine Gast

COUNCIL *on* **FOUNDATIONS**

VISION

The Council's vision for the field is of

A vibrant, growing and responsible philanthropic sector that advances the common good.

We see ourselves as part of a broad philanthropic community that will contribute to this vision. We aim to be an important leader in reaching the vision.

MISSION

The Council on Foundations provides the opportunity, leadership and tools needed by philanthropic organizations to expand, enhance and sustain their ability to advance the common good.

To carry out this mission, we will be a membership organization with effective and diverse leadership that helps the field be larger, more effective, more responsible and more cooperative.

By "*common good*," we mean the sum total of conditions that enable community members to thrive. These achievements have a shared nature that goes beyond individual benefits.

By "*philanthropic organizations*," we mean any vehicle that brings people together to enhance the effectiveness, impact and leverage of their philanthropy. This includes private and community foundations, corporate foundations and giving programs, operating foundations and public foundations, as well as emerging giving and grantmaking mechanisms involving collective participation.

STATEMENT OF INCLUSIVENESS

The Council on Foundations was formed to promote responsible and effective philanthropy. The mission requires a commitment to inclusiveness as a fundamental operating principle and calls for an active and ongoing process that affirms human diversity in its many forms, encompassing but not limited to ethnicity, race, gender, sexual orientation, economic circumstance, disability and philosophy. We seek diversity in order to ensure that a range of perspectives, opinions and experiences are recognized and acted upon in achieving the Council's mission. The Council also asks members to make a similar commitment to inclusiveness in order to better enhance their abilities to contribute to the common good of our changing society.

Library of Congress Cataloging-in-Publication Data

Gast, Elaine.
 Built on principle : a guide to family foundation stewardship / written by Elaine Gast.
    p. cm.
 ISBN 1-932677-06-2
 1. Family foundations—United States—Management. I. Council on Foundations. II. Title.
 HV97.A3G368 2006
 361.7'632--dc22
                              2005037065

COUNCIL on FOUNDATIONS
1828 L Street, NW, Suite 300
Washington, DC 20036-5168
202/466-6512 • Fax 202/785-3926
www.cof.org

TABLE OF CONTENTS

ACKNOWLEDGMENTS

To the Council on Foundations Committee on Family Foundations, for giving voice to the needs of family foundations.

To the Advisory Group for Family Foundation and Corporate Grantmaking Principles, for supporting the development of the Stewardship Principles.

To the Stewardship Principles Editorial Review Committee, whose vision and foundation experience shaped this book.

Editorial Review Committee Members

Jean Buckley, President, Tracy Family Foundation
Christine Elbel, Executive Director, Fleishhacker Foundation
Taylor Jordan, Board Member, Cricket Island Foundation
Robert N. Mayer, Ph.D., Treasurer, The Nathan Cummings Foundation
Olivia Maynard, Trustee, Charles Stewart Mott Foundation

PREFACE

Although the earliest family foundations were created decades ago, the field has grown significantly in scope and energy in recent years and has become an influential force for society, providing resources beyond money, including leadership, time, talent and commitment. With the increasing numbers has come a growing need for family foundations to have guiding principles and effective practices. It was for this reason that the Council on Foundations embarked on a partnership with the field to develop the Stewardship Principles for Family Foundations.

These principles and practice options help family foundations operate in ways that meet the standards for ethics and accountability appropriate to the public trust. They help boards and staff build the capacity to fulfill their missions. They also demonstrate to Congress and our communities that we are an ethical and well-run field and have been for decades.

This book offers detailed guidance on ways foundations can achieve each of the nine Stewardship Principles. We've canvassed the family foundation field to find models, examples, sample documents and other tools that have worked for your peers and can help you improve your own foundation performance.

Built on Principle is a compilation of the field's collective wisdom. We hope you find this publication useful in dealing with the many philosophical and practical issues all family foundations face while pursuing the noble cause of philanthropy.

Susan C. Price
Managing Director, Family Foundation Services
Council on Foundations

INTRODUCTION

"The Stewardship Principles are expressions of family foundations trying to be the best they can be. They help all of us who run family foundations think about what we could do but are not yet doing."

—Bill O'Neill Jr., president of the William J. and Dorothy K. O'Neill Foundation

Family foundations are private foundations in which the donor or the donor's relatives play a significant governing role. Their roles and responsibilities are similar to other grantmakers but with the added dimension of family involvement. This book is designed to help all family foundations achieve excellence, no matter their asset size, staff composition or board structure.

The book centers on a set of nine Stewardship Principles and Practice Options formulated to assist board members in exercising strong governance, ethics and accountability, all while honoring their families' legacies. Adopted by the Council on Foundations Committee on Family Foundations in September 2004, the principles were the product of more than a year's worth of work and input from the field. Each of the nine principles could easily have an entire book devoted to it—and some of them do. What you will read here is a basic overview. Resources provided at the end of each chapter will give you more detailed information on each topic.

Each chapter features an introduction to the principle, along with examples from the field located in side-bars titled Peer Practices and In Their Own Words. At the end of each chapter, you'll find the actual samples and tools your colleagues have found to be most helpful. You can use these samples as they are or adapt them to meet your own foundation's needs.

Using this book as a framework, your family foundation board and staff can discuss issues before they arise. Think of it as a planning tool, allowing you to develop thoughtful policy and practices that improve over time.

The practice options aren't intended to be items on a checklist, although you may find it helpful to use them that way. They also aren't meant to be static. Just as your foundation grows and changes, so will the way you implement the principles. And remember, the practice options are just that—options. They aren't prescriptive, nor are they appropriate for every foundation.

How you use the principles and practice options will depend on your asset size, staff, board composition, culture and other factors. Although you may not be ready or able to fully implement all of these principles and practice options *now*—this book will give you ideas for when you are.

> *"Before [the Stewardship Principles], family foundations were like the old song 'I Did It My Way'."*
>
> *—Bruce Maza, executive director of the C.E. & S. Foundation*

Who Should Read This Book

Anyone in your family foundation—large or small, staffed or board-managed—can use this book to reflect on and improve current practice. That said, this book speaks most directly to those in leadership roles. Different people fill these roles in different foundations—the donor, board chair, officer or trustee, or perhaps the executive director or foundation manager.

No matter your title or responsibilities, this book will help you bring the principles and practice options to your board to discuss and implement, as appropriate.

A note on terminology: The members of a board may be known as board members, directors or trustees depending on the structure of the foundation. These terms are used interchangeably in this book, as well as in the philanthropic community.

The Origin of the Stewardship Principles

In 2002, a Council survey of family foundations revealed that 94 percent of respondents wanted a set of guiding principles. Like others in the charitable community, the field wanted a means to improve its governance, management and grantmaking.

To respond to that need, the Council's Committee on Family Foundations and the Family Foundation Services Department embarked on a yearlong project to devise principles and practice options promoting good governance, ethics and accountability, while honoring family legacy. As part of the process, the Council welcomed input from hundreds of family foundations to ensure a real-world perspective.

After a listening tour in seven cities, and dozens of drafts, the Committee on Family Foundations approved the Stewardship Principles and Practice Options to Strengthen Performance, with the unanimous support of the Council on Foundations Board of Directors. All of the work took place with the guidance of an advisory group, composed of family and corporate foundation executives and trustees, and experts including academics, attorneys and an ethicist.

Words of Advice from Your Colleagues

"Principles" sounds like lofty ideals—something to strive for, but hard to achieve in real life. By learning and applying the tools in this book, however, you'll find how simple—and accessible—the principles really are.

Still, if you're like most foundations, you might be looking at the Stewardship Principles and thinking, "Now what?"

Good question. The principles cover such a wide range of topics and possible practices that they can be overwhelming at first glance. But they don't have to be.

"When I took the Stewardship Principles to our board, I didn't even know how to start the conversation," said Anna Kay Frueauff of the Frueauff Foundation. "I realized we couldn't possibly accomplish them all in one massive chunk—we had to take it one principle at a time."

Some family foundations have begun discussing the Stewardship Principles and how to apply them. Here are some ideas from your colleagues:

- *Compare the practice options to your current practices.* Bill O'Neill, president of the O'Neill Foundation, examined all of the practice options in the Stewardship Principles and determined that his family foundation already does 85 percent. "It showed us a lot of the things we had already done were pointed in the right direction," said O'Neill. "It also showed us where the holes were and what we could do better."

- *Survey the board.* "Using the 'Governance' section of the Stewardship Principles, I drafted a survey and sent it to our board," said Anna Kay Frueauff, trustee of the Charles A. Frueauff Foundation. In the survey, board members were asked to assign a number to how well the board addressed each of the principles. "I got the surveys back, tallied the results and sorted them in terms of what got the highest and lowest ratings. That gave us a handful of things to address—some substance that we could work on and change." The process led the board to hold a retreat, which, according to Frueauff, they don't usually do. "Now, we'll have one next summer as well."

- *Use the principles and options to stimulate board discussion.* "Every board is struggling with something different at different times. We used the Stewardship Principles to organize topics at a board retreat and prioritize what was important to us," said Kathleen Odne, executive director of the Dean and Margaret Lesher Foundation. "The practice

"The Stewardship Principles are excellent—but you have to do more than just read them."

—Anna Kay Frueauff, trustee,
Charles A. Frueauff Foundation

"In this process, it's important not to focus just on what you need to work on, but to affirm what you are doing right. People will be more willing to make change...if you fill the well first."

—Kathleen Odne, executive director, Dean and Margaret Lesher Foundation

options serve as good discussion entry points—where we could see what we were already doing and how we might apply the suggested practices to some of our initiatives. It was time well worth spending, and for us, it was a way of seeing that we've really already done a lot."

- *Support the Stewardship Principles.* The Weaver Foundation's website states that it subscribes to the Stewardship Principles and includes a link to them on the Council's website. "We want to hold ourselves up as believing in the principles," said Skip Moore, executive director. "We treat them as a framework for self-study."

- *Give positive reinforcement.* "Because my board has already undertaken many of these practices, I'm using them as a 'pat on the back,' to commend them for being proactive," said Caroline Sabin, executive director of The Powell Foundation in Houston. "Family foundations should continue to revisit the document often, since the community's needs change. The Stewardship Principles will provide them with a good framework to think through those needs effectively."

With countless options facing your family foundation, there is no "one right way" to approach the Stewardship Principles. Nor is this a one-time job. At every stage, your board must make choices—and anticipate the effects of those choices.

This book, and the options herein, will help you. Enjoy.

STEWARDSHIP PRINCIPLES FOR FAMILY FOUNDATIONS

GOVERNANCE

I. We have a governing board that establishes the mission, guides the operations, oversees the effectiveness and ensures the ethical conduct of the foundation.

II. Authority is vested in the governing board as a whole, and each member is equipped to advance the foundation's mission.

III. We consider multiple strategies to further our mission.

IV. Our governing board exercises active fiscal oversight.

ETHICS AND ACCOUNTABILITY

V. We recognize and act upon our obligations to multiple stakeholders: the donor and the donor's family, grantees and grantseekers, the public and governmental bodies.

VI. We respect our nonprofit partners' missions and expertise and strive for relationships based on candor, understanding and fairness.

VII. We welcome public interest and communicate openly.

FAMILY LEGACY

VIII. Our governing board respects donor intent and later generations' interests while also considering the demands of a changing world.

IX. We plan for family leadership continuity.

These nine principles expand to include Practice Options to Strengthen Performance, a selection of practices that family foundations can discuss and follow as appropriate.

Adopted by the Committee on Family Foundations, September 2004

PART I: GOVERNANCE

We have a governing board that establishes the mission, guides the operations, oversees the effectiveness and ensures the ethical conduct of the foundation. Authority is vested in the governing board as a whole, and each member is equipped to advance the foundation's mission. We consider multiple strategies to further our mission. Our governing board exercises active fiscal oversight. **We recognize and act upon our obligations to multiple stakeholders: the donor and the donor's family, grantees and grantseekers, the public and governmental bodies.** We respect our nonprofit partners' missions and expertise and strive for relationships based on candor, understanding and fairness. We welcome public interest and communicate openly. **Our governing board respects donor intent and later generations' interests while also considering the demands of a changing world.** We plan for family leadership continuity. We have a governing board that establishes the mission, guides the operations, oversees the effectiveness and ensures the ethical conduct of the foundation. Authority is vested in the governing board as a whole, and each member is equipped to advance the foundation's mission. **We consider multiple strategies to further our mission.** Our governing board exercises active fiscal oversight. We recognize and act upon our obligations to multiple stakeholders: the donor and the donor's family, grantees and grantseekers, the public and governmental bodies. **We respect our nonprofit partners' missions and expertise and strive for relationships based on candor, understanding and fairness.** We welcome public interest and communicate openly. Our governing board respects donor intent and later generations' interests while also considering the demands of a changing world. We plan for family leadership continuity. **We have a governing board that establishes the mission, guides the operations, oversees the effectiveness and ensures the ethical conduct of the foundation.** Authority is vested in the governing board as a whole, and each member is equipped to advance the foundation's mission. We consider multiple strategies to further our mission. **Our governing board exercises active fiscal oversight.** We recognize and act upon our obligations to multiple stakeholders: the donor and the donor's family, grantees and grantseekers, the public and governmental bodies. We respect our nonprofit partners' missions and expertise and strive for relationships based on candor, understanding and fairness. **We welcome public interest and communicate openly.** Our governing board respects donor intent and later generations' interests while also considering the demands of a changing world. **We plan for family leadership continuity.** We have a governing board that establishes the mission, guides the operations, oversees the effectiveness and ensures the ethical conduct of the foundation. **Authority is vested in the governing board as a whole, and each member is equipped to advance the foundation's mission.** We consider multiple strategies to further our mission. Our governing board exercises active fiscal oversight. We recognize and act upon our obligations to multiple stake-

CHAPTER 1
Lead Your Foundation

PRINCIPLE I:

WE HAVE A GOVERNING BOARD THAT ESTABLISHES THE MISSION, GUIDES THE OPERATIONS, OVERSEES THE EFFECTIVENESS AND ENSURES THE ETHICAL CONDUCT OF THE FOUNDATION.

Family foundation is not a legal term and therefore has no precise definition. Yet, nearly two-fifths of the foundations in this country are believed to be family managed.

The Council on Foundations defines a family foundation as one in which a significant governing role is played by the donor or the donor's relatives. Family foundations share a common heritage: They were formed by a donor or family of donors, most likely with resources from a family business, investments or inheritance. These donors established foundations for a number of reasons. Perhaps they were committed to the family and to something larger than the family. Perhaps they wanted to leave a legacy, a mark of how they made a difference. Or perhaps they wanted to give back to the community that helped them thrive.

Family foundations work on matters they care about with people they care about. They do this by serving on a governing board.

> ### IN THIS CHAPTER
>
> - Develop your values, vision, mission
> - Find the human, financial and technology resources to meet your mission
> - Plan for leadership continuity
> - Assess your foundation's effectiveness.

The governing board is the cornerstone of your family foundation—the body that has ultimate authority over the organization. The board sets forth a statement of purpose and then works together, allocating funds to meet that purpose. Governance refers to how your board "steers" the foundation.

The governing board is responsible for the most essential of foundation operations—establishing the mission, managing the finances, guiding the operations and overseeing the effectiveness and ethical conduct of the foundation. Board members have important legal and fiduciary responsibilities that require a commitment of time and skills.

Family foundation boards are as different from one another as the causes and communities they serve. They operate differently, they make grants differently, and they approach their work differently. Each celebrates its own distinct family history, culture, values, resources and leadership style.

But family foundations do have one thing in common: The foundation is only as good as its governing board. For you to sustain the organization, make effective grants and meet your mission, you must have an effective governing body. This can be easier said than done, as serving on a family foundation board is no easy task.

This book provides you with principles and practices that will help you and your board. Chapter 1 provides an overview of your board's roles and responsibilities. In some sections, it points to other chapters where you can learn about these roles in greater detail.

PRACTICE OPTIONS FOR PRINCIPLE I

A. DEVELOP AND PERIODICALLY REVIEW THE FOUNDATION'S VALUES AND MISSION STATEMENT, STRATEGIES, PROGRAM AREAS AND GUIDELINES, GOALS, ANNUAL AND MULTIYEAR OBJECTIVES AND GEOGRAPHIC FOCUS.

At its core, a foundation exists to change the world, or at least some part of it. Family foundations work to make something happen that wouldn't happen otherwise. In doing so, they bring the family together to work around a cause, in a way most families never do.

Viewed this way, the task of setting forth a foundation's direction can seem formidable. It helps to think in terms of the core values, vision and mission—the guiding principles behind your foundation. Let's take a look at what these mean:

Your values statement describes your foundation's core principles and culture. A values statement informs your work—how you interact with others in the community and among your own board, staff and volunteers. *What overall philosophy and ethics guide you? How do trustees interact, with each other and with the community?*

Your vision statement describes your foundation's aspirations—what you hope to accomplish in the future. Through its vision statement, your foundation defines its motivation for existing—its ultimate dreams and image for an ideal world. *What do you aspire to? What would a better world look like?*

Your mission defines the purpose of your foundation's philanthropy—what you hope to accomplish in the present to bring about your vision for the future. The mission statement clarifies the reason for your foundation's being. It describes the needs it was created to fill, and specifies what geographic area you serve. *Why do you exist? What areas/causes/regions will you fund to bring about your vision for the future?*

Every organization needs to define the values, vision and mission that drive what it does. Consider these statements the spinal column of your foundation—the cord that connects all other limbs of your foundation's program. All day-to-day activities flow from this cord.

Of these three statements, the one you hear about most is the mission. Perhaps that's because while your values and vision may be somewhat aspirational, the mission defines your purpose and what you can do today. A mission is tangible and at the same time, motivational.

Your mission can, and should, serve as your continuous "check in" throughout your decisionmaking—your way for the foundation to stay grounded in its values and vision. It also gives you something by which to assess how well your foundation works, and how much of a difference you make.

Just as people and communities change, so too can mission statements. That's why it's important to regularly review your foundation's mission to make sure it is still relevant.

If you periodically review the mission statement, you can verify that you're on the right track and making good decisions—or perhaps realize that the mission no longer serves the foundation or the community you serve. Build mission review into your board's yearly operating schedule, and it will become a regular part of business.

Here are some questions to guide you as you review your mission, strategies and more:

- How is our mission relevant and effective?

- Is our mission statement grounded in our values? If not, what is missing?

- Does the statement communicate to the average person who we are and what we do? Does it encompass all the people we want to serve?

- Is the statement long and abstract, or short and snappy?

- How are we "making a difference"?

- Is this a mission we're excited about and proud of? If not, what can be done?

- Has the donor defined his or her intent for the foundation? What flexibility does the board have to alter that intent?

- If necessary, how could we change the mission to better meet the needs of the community? To better meet the needs of the family?

When defining or reviewing your mission, it might be best to have the discussion outside of a regular board business meeting. For example, you might hold a facilitated family retreat to discuss board member ideologies and interests. You might also seek advice or assistance from grantmaking professionals at other family foundations who have perhaps been through the process themselves.

Once you are clear on your mission, you can use it to articulate your program strategies. Strategies lay out your plan for reaching your mission. *What do you want to accomplish? How will you get from here to there?* Your board will likely develop its strategies in its strategic planning process. This is where the board designs its goals, short- and long-term objectives, methods and (if you haven't done so already) your grant guidelines. *See chapter 6 for more on developing grant guidelines.*

Quick Tip

Post your foundation's values, vision and mission statement on the wall of your board meeting room and on top of the board meeting agenda. Refer to these statements often as a group to keep your foundation's larger purpose front and center in every discussion.

In Their Own Words

What Our Mission Means to Us

"Our mission statement is a shorthand reminder of what informs and energizes our actions and of what we bring to the conversations with those whom we seek to affect. Such shorthand is useful only in a context of common understanding; the process of communication requires as much attention as the process of discovery. In our annual report and other publications we present not only the mission, but also our goals, guidelines, values, strategies, practices and history, which together form the context for the mission and express our vision of what we try to accomplish. Our success depends on communicating our purpose in such a way that it speaks to the condition of those whose actions will change the world."

—William Graustein, trustees, William Caspar Graustein Memorial Fund

Peer Practices

Retreats Bring Big Picture Results

The Hamilton-White Foundation in San Diego, planned and ran two board retreats. The first, in 2001, focused on values, vision and mission of the foundation and the message the foundation wanted to convey to the community it served. During the retreat, board members conveyed their passions and inspirations for philanthropic service. The second retreat, 18 months later in 2003, further refined and refocused the foundations vision and mission, and the board discussed more strategic grantmaking issues.

Former President Phil White advised other boards, when conducting similar retreats, to keep focused on big picture results. "The agenda should not be overly complicated or too complex to cover in the time allotted," said White. "Try to move quickly along so board members don't get bogged down in details or drift off topic during discussions."

B. DEDICATE SUFFICIENT HUMAN, FINANCIAL AND TECHNOLOGICAL RESOURCES TO ADVANCE THE MISSION.

Whether you have a new or established foundation, your board must make sure the proper human, financial and technology resources are in place. Otherwise, how will you pursue your mission?

Every family foundation manages its operations differently. Some foundations operate with a mix of full- or part-time staff, board members, consultants and committees. Others run their foundation from their dining room table, without the luxury of a staff or foundation office.

Both modes of operation are perfectly legitimate, and which path your foundation follows will likely depend on its size and growth stage. Like running any organization, though, your foundation needs sufficient human, financial and technological resources to be effective—if not now, than certainly in the future.

Human Resources

You will need *someone* to manage the foundation. A foundation manager or executive director helps the foundation make the best use of its assets. Good management affects the entire organization and leads to good governance, good strategic planning and good grantmaking.

When a foundation first starts out, the donor (or donor couple) usually assumes this role or delegates the role to a family friend or associate. As time goes on, the board might decide to hire paid staff, an outside consultant (individual or firm) or a board member to serve as staff (*see chapter 5 on the self-dealing rules*). Staff should be chosen carefully for their competence, experience and skills with respect to professional relations, nonprofits or the foundation's field of interest. Some foundations use a search firm to diversity their search or if they don't have the time or ability to conduct a thorough themselves.

When a board hires staff for the first time, board members must make the critical transition from a "working board" to a "policy board." As the board separates policy from staff functions, confusion in roles may arise. To assist in this time of transition, help your board understand its roles and responsibilities and the separate and joint roles of staff. Offer your board sample job descriptions and describe the different roles of board and staff.

Below is a list of typical board and staff member roles.

Who Leads the Foundation?

Here's a basic overview of various board and staff roles:

THE BOARD CHAIR:

The chair (also called chairperson or board president) leads the board. As the chief volunteer officer, the board chair presides over meetings, rallies the board, supports the executive director/foundation administrator and facilitates communication between the board and the staff. Board chairs facilitate the foundation's direction.

BOARD OFFICERS:

Board officers usually include a vice chair, treasurer and/or secretary and on some boards, the executive director. Together, this leadership team shoulders specific board responsibilities.

EXECUTIVE DIRECTOR (ALSO CALLED FOUNDATION MANAGER OR ADMINISTRATOR):

Typically, the executive director oversees the daily and long-term operations of the foundation, according to with the board's directives. Responsibilities may include hiring staff (if any) and defining job responsibilities, overseeing programs and costs, establishing a financial infrastructure, planning and coordinating board meetings, initiating the board's strategic planning process, communicating fully and frequently with the board and acting in a leadership capacity on behalf of the foundation.

The Staff (if any):

Depending on the foundation's stage of growth, the executive director may hire staff members to fill certain roles. Staff roles might include programming (grants), finance, communications and administration.

Financial Resources

When you join a foundation board, you are what's called a fiduciary—a steward of the foundation's assets. As a fiduciary, you have a responsibility to invest money and act wisely on behalf of the foundation. It's your job to make sure your foundation complies with federal, state and local laws.

As a foundation board member, you have two primary roles in managing the foundation's assets: a fiscal responsibility and an investment responsibility.

Fiscal responsibility involves developing and approving the budget, monitoring financial performance, making sure tax returns are filed correctly, ensuring internal controls are in place, and making sure the foundation follows the law.

Investment responsibility includes overseeing the investment process—developing policies and strategies, reviewing the foundation's portfolio performance, and more.

Chapter 4 goes into more detail on how your board can exercise active fiscal oversight.

Technology

Technology can help you manage your foundation. Whether you operate from a full-scale networked office or from a laptop on your kitchen table, you need technology to support your mission.

Although technology is never a replacement for face-to-face communication, it helps foundations take care of routine business. Many boards use e-mail, the telephone and the Web to schedule and plan board meetings, keep grantseekers and the community informed, and even pre-screen proposals.

Start planning for technology by assessing what operations you need to support. Consider how technology can help you in the following areas:

- Grants management
- Accounting and financial/tax reporting
- Investment management
- Budgeting
- Communicating via a website
- Scheduling (for example, tracking board and other meetings)

Once you are more aware of the foundation's overall needs, you can then begin your search. It may help to get advice from other foundations or nonprofit organizations of a similar size and region.

Many foundations use grants management software to support their grantmaking function. Typically, the software provides the framework for tracking and analyzing grant requests and the supporting data that accompanies the requests. It ensures quality control and data integrity necessary for your foundation's accountability. Plus it can make your foundation manager's job a whole lot easier. If you are considering this type of software, make sure it supports the goals of your foundation. Talk to your colleagues to see what works for them.

One type of technology you should consider is a website. Websites express your mission and communicate your guidelines to potential grantees—helping to ensure applications come in that are consistent with your mission. Websites have a practical side as well: They can help you communicate with your board (*See the sidebar Technology Helps Trustees Stay Informed*). If you aren't ready to design your own site, the Foundation Center offers a Web service for foundations (called Foundation Folders). To find out more, visit www.fdncenter.org, or contact 212/807-2481. *See chapter 7 for more on developing a website.*

As you're thinking about what you need in terms of technology, consider the costs in dollars, staff time, training, licensing and more. Depending on your foundation's strategy, size and budget, you should be able to come up with a technology solution that will work well.

Remember, though, that adding technology isn't a one-time event. As time goes on, your foundation may change, and your operating systems will need updating. It helps to keep lists of the equipment and software you use for when you do need to update your system.

Peer Practices

Technology Helps Trustees Stay Informed

The Nord Family Foundation created a private section on its public website to keep the 30-plus members informed and engaged in the foundation. Family members and trustees use passwords to access information on foundation operations, grant requests and resources. "Our ultimate goal," said executive director John Mullaney, is to use this information for more informed trustee meetings, more responsible grantmaking and a clearer understanding of the administrative issues that staff and trustees must address. The site features information, bylaws, committee tasks and a finance section. The foundation added a blog section, where trustees can post comments and receive responses.

In addition to the family website, the foundation is initiating a feedback loop, in which they invite the public to post comments about issues of concern in their program areas. They also invite feedback on how the foundation is doing in response to community needs.

C. Plan for leadership continuity.

Until now, your foundation may have had only one leader—you (if you are the founder). As time goes by, however, your family will need a good system for choosing new leaders. This choice may be obvious or difficult. As families grow, there may be many candidates—sometimes more than the foundation can accommodate. And small families may have the opposite problem—not enough family members to take on the job.

You (or the founder) started the foundation with certain goals in mind. No doubt, those goals are still important as you think about your foundation's future. To ensure a smooth transition as your foundation evolves, plan ahead.

Here are some ways to start planning for leadership continuity now:

Develop a clear mission statement and share the rationale with your family. *What parts of your foundation's mission and grantmaking priorities need to remain constant for the foundation to retain its character and connection to the founder? What parts have the potential to evolve?*

Discuss your goals for the foundation with your family. This will help them understand what matters to you, the deeper reasons behind the everyday activities of philanthropy. *Do you want the foundation to exist in perpetuity? Is it a priority to see your children take over when you're gone?*

Talk with potential successors about the history of the foundation. Share how you got involved in giving and how your goals relate to your ancestors and community. This will not only help prepare future foundation leaders for their roles, but it will also provide you with fresh perspectives.

Involve successors in grantmaking activities to help teach your history and philosophy firsthand. Use a site visit to explain to your children what matters to you. Seek the help and advice of younger generations.

Keep track of your history. Having a record of the past of both your family and your foundation will help you lay the groundwork for the future. Consider keeping a family foundation history, photographs, donor letters or videos, annual reports and archives.

Learn from other families. Many families already have been through leadership transitions, and can share their lessons learned. Contact the Council's Family Foundation Services (family@cof.org) for ideas on whom to contact.

As part of your planning, you should create (or update) board member job descriptions.

Job descriptions are one of the best tools for board effectiveness and for succession. They brief new board members on the purpose, responsibilities, duties and rationale for each board position.

For more on leadership continuity, see chapters 8 and 9. For more on job descriptions, see chapter 2.

D. ASSESS THE RELEVANCE AND EFFECTIVENESS OF THE FOUNDATION'S GRANTMAKING, BOARD GOVERNANCE, MANAGEMENT AND INVESTMENTS.

As part of its responsibility, a board strengthens what works and abandons what doesn't. Good boards regularly assess themselves and their work. Encourage your board to assess the relevance and effectiveness of its work in the areas of grantmaking, governance, management and investments. Remind the board that assessment is nothing to fear—in fact, it can be a tremendous growth opportunity.

Ideally you will want to conduct an assessment once a year, but no less often than every two to three years. When assessing your work, you will likely want to focus on one area of your foundation at a time. For example, one time you might formally evaluate your grants program and the next time your governance structure and board performance. This is not to say that you won't continually monitor *all* areas of your foundation throughout the year. But to make the most of your evaluations—and not overwhelm yourselves in the process—it helps to focus on one area at a time.

Boards sometimes hire an outside facilitator for the assessment process. Facilitators might interview individual board members and sometimes staff or hold an all-day board retreat for evaluation as a group. Other boards choose to keep evaluation simple by conducting a self-assessment. The board chair, or an ad-hoc assessment committee, might administer surveys to members and then discuss the results with the board as a whole.

In a self-assessment process, your board members should begin by evaluating their work as a group. Suggest that your board discuss the following sample questions.

Questions for the Entire Board

- How is the mission relevant?
- How is the board structure effective? How could it be improved?
- Who is our primary "customer?"
- How well do board members know their roles and organizational relationships?

- What can our board do to improve its work?
- How well does our board communicate with stakeholders?
- How well does our board perform in leadership and planning activities?
- What board development and organizational capacity building does the board do?
- How well does the board report and document procedures?
- How prepared is the board? What is the level of member participation?
- How well does the board know the community or fields it funds?

Next, board members should evaluate their own individual performance, and/or that of their peers. Some boards use a simple and confidential survey format, asking members to rate themselves on items using a scale of one to five. On any survey, it helps to also include open-ended questions to get a range of responses.

Questions for Individual Board Members

- How well do I understand and support the mission?
- How well do I understand my roles and responsibilities?
- How well do I prepare in advance?
- Do I regularly attend and participate in meetings? Events? Site visits?
- Do I volunteer for committees and serve effectively on them?
- Do I recommend individuals for board service?
- Do I participate in professional development?
- How valuable do I find board service?
- What could I do to improve my effectiveness?

As part of evaluation, board members might ask for feedback on their performance. As behavioral science has shown, feedback has an uncanny effect on performance. Sometimes knowing that performance will be evaluated can prompt a positive change in behavior.

Tool for Board Effectiveness

The Center for Effective Philanthropy is now making its Comparative Board Report (CBR)— a self-assessment tool for improving board effectiveness—broadly available to foundations. The CBR, which was tested by more than 50 foundations, presents comparative data on board member perceptions, as well as board structures and practices, based on confidential surveys of foundation trustees and CEOs. The CBR process takes approximately 10 weeks to complete and assists CEOs and trustees with informed and guided conversations about their own performance. Read more at www.effectivephilanthropy.com.

In Their Own Words

Board Exit Interviews

"At the end of 2000, the terms of four long-term foundation board members expired. We thought it would be useful for an outside consultant to conduct an interview of the four to assess their experiences on the board and obtain their recommendations to help the board operate more effectively. At the end of 2004, we also had four board members leave and did another set of exit interviews—this time, conducted by the board chair.

"Among the questions asked were:

- What are the achievements you are most proud of?
- Did the board's effectiveness change over the years?
- At the end of your term were you comfortable about the direction of the foundation?
- Do you think the foundation is addressing the right issues?
- What are your hopes for the board's future and what advice do you have?

"Based on the earlier interviews, some of the exiting board members suggested we do a better job in board training and orientations. As a result of this suggestion, we put together a board handbook, began a mentorship program for new board members and give new members an opportunity to meet with the staff as a part of their orientation."

—Victor De Luca, president, Jessie Smith Noyes Foundation

How Do You Measure Success?

"The founders started the foundation so that the family could do collective philanthropy. They wanted to create a formal structure through which the children and grandchildren could continue to work together. So, in addition to achieving particular goals in our grantmaking area, success, to us, means having the family active and involved."

—Julie Simpson, executive director, Cricket Island Foundation

In sum, ask yourselves:

- Am I an active, knowledgeable trustee?

- Do I understand my foundation's mission, programs and strategic plan?

- Am I, and is the foundation, devoting enough time and resources to help the foundation achieve its mission?

- When was the last time we assessed the performance of the board of directors, staff and program areas?

Resources

The Family Advisor: Values, Vision, and Mission. Council on Foundations. Visit www.cof.org.

The Family Foundation Library Series. Council on Foundations, 1997. Item #815.
Visit www.cof.org/publications.

Family Matters newsletter: "Assessing our Work" *(Summer 2001) and "Values at Play" (Fall 2000).*
Visit www.cof.org.

The Guide to Small Foundation Management: From Groundwork to Grantmaking. Council on Foundations 2002. Item #827. Visit www.cof.org/publications.

SAMPLE DOCUMENTS FOR PRINCIPLE I

Sample Values Statement
Courtesy of the Ken W. Davis Foundation

As members, officers and directors of the Ken W. Davis Foundation, we believe our effectiveness is based on our values for discovering the potential for partnerships and building productive relationships. These relationships should involve continuous learning and teaching by both the foundation and the partner organization. We accept our responsibilities as leaders and each strive to:

Relationships

- Treat others as we wish to be treated, with humility, dignity, respect and honesty
- Work inclusively and collaboratively with others
- Encourage results
- Maintain commitment to excellence in achieving results
- Pursue creativity and take responsible risks
- Seek renewal
- Engage in lifelong learning through personal and professional development
- Seek balance with career and personal life

Sample Values Statement
Courtesy of the Halcyon Hill Foundation, www.hhf.org

The values that drive the philanthropic mission of Halcyon Hill are many. Energy curiosity, and participation define the commitment of the foundation; loyalty, respect and sensitivity, its integrity; a strong belief in collaboration, innovation and leadership speak to its sense of community responsibility; and finally, the wish for good humor, quietude and graciousness characterize all aspects of its decisionmaking.

With these values in mind, the founder's children are continuing the philanthropy that their mother began, working toward peace, tranquility and enriched opportunities for Rochester's children.

Sample Mission and Beliefs Statement

Courtesy of the Mary Reynolds Babcock Foundation

The Mary Reynolds Babcock Foundation assists people in the Southeast to build just and caring communities that nurture people, spur enterprise, bridge differences and foster fairness. Our mission is to help people and places to move out of poverty and achieve greater social and economic justice. We support organizations and networks that work across race, ethnic, economic and political differences to make possible a brighter future for all.

We believe in the responsibility and power of individuals—including youth and young adults—to improve their own lives and to act collectively to increase opportunity for themselves and their communities. All human beings have the potential to be productive citizens, yet individual responsibility is not enough. Social and economic transformation in low-wealth communities requires changes in historic disinvestment patterns and removal of structural barriers.

We value democracy and inclusiveness. We believe in working with people in low-wealth communities to shape their own destiny. We believe that working across differences is essential for sustaining our democracy and for expanding economic opportunity.

We hold the following beliefs about how people and places move out of poverty:

- Ownership of **assets** such as homes, businesses and savings is essential for moving and staying out of poverty.

- People have better chances at building assets when they **believe** in themselves, make good **choices**, and have **access** to fundamental opportunities (e.g. excellent education, social networks that connect them to work and to the larger society, living-wage jobs and fair financial institutions.)

- These basic societal advantages require a solid **infrastructure** and consistent **investment**. In order to secure these advantages in low-wealth communities, changes in systems and policies—local, state and/or national—are almost always necessary. Long-term public and private investment is also essential.

- **Connections** are vital. Grassroots, community-led organizations must be connected with key institutions in their states, the Southeast or across the nation in order to achieve large-scale, lasting changes. On a bigger level, local economies must be connected to regional economies.

- **Young people** can take on leadership roles that improve their own lives, make contributions to their communities and prepare them for lives of active citizenship.

- Large-scale, lasting change requires **skilled individuals** and **effective organizations** working for social and economic justice with a broad range of allies.

- Change takes **time**. Changing the conditions that cause persistent poverty is incremental, non-linear and long-term work that is dependent upon a combination of sound strategy, serendipity and intuition.

The Foundation seeks partners who share our mission and beliefs, and we honor the impact, integrity and creativity of people across our region already engaged in this work. We make grants to local, statewide and regional nonprofits in the Southeastern United States that have track records of helping low-wealth people build assets and transform economic conditions in their communities.

CHAPTER 2
Lead and Learn Collectively

PRINCIPLE II:

AUTHORITY IS VESTED IN THE GOVERNING BOARD AS A WHOLE, AND EACH MEMBER IS EQUIPPED TO ADVANCE THE FOUNDATION'S MISSION.

Serving on a family foundation board is both a terrific honor and a great responsibility. As you learned in chapter 1, board members must understand their legal responsibilities in governing the foundation. A good board stays well informed and uses good judgment. Members put aside personal and professional interests for the good of the organization. Moreover, they ensure that the foundation stays true to its mission and purpose.

In short, the board is in charge of the foundation—the entire board.

A board can exercise its governing power only as an entity—not as individual members. Although individuals may act as special advisors or offer expertise on certain issues, board members can only set policy and make important decisions when acting as a full board.

That said, each member of the board should be individually prepared and equipped to advance the foundation's mission, and each needs certain guidelines, training and tools to do this.

Chapter 2 will help you give your board what it needs to lead and to learn.

IN THIS CHAPTER

- Develop your values, vision, mission
- Set criteria for board composition and membership
- Craft bylaws
- Conduct regular meetings
- Stay on mission
- Orient new members
- Provide continuing education for the board.

Practice Options for Principle II

A. Identify the desired characteristics of the governing board, including size, composition and member skills and experience; consider diversity and the perspective offered by representatives from outside the family.

Family foundation boards come in all shapes, sizes and personalities. Many foundations start with small boards—perhaps the founder, the spouse or adult child or children, and a legal advisor. Over the years, as the next generation comes of age and the donor leaves the scene, the board might expand to accommodate the number of adult family members. Eventually, the foundation board may grow into a larger group, complete with aunts and uncles, cousins and community members.

One theme you'll find running through this book is to plan ahead. It may seem obvious, but setting guidelines for your board now will pay big dividends in the future. It helps to be mindful of the desired characteristics of your board and its members—and put your desires in writing. Look to your mission, and ask yourselves:

- What are we trying to accomplish?
- What size and structure do we need to get the job done?
- What skills and expertise do we need on the board?
- Who will be eligible for board service?

Board Size and Structure

The size and structure of your board should reflect your mission and the needs of your community. There is no ideal board size, although some states do require a minimum size for nonprofit boards (usually three). Some boards prefer to stay small, while others see the value in a large board with many perspectives.

It helps to state in writing a minimum and maximum number for your board, if not already written in your bylaws or articles of incorporation. Some boards opt for an uneven number of members to prevent tie votes. Whatever size you choose, be sure to include the rationale for your decision to inform future members. You might include a statement in your policy allowing the board size to adjust over the years, to meet changing conditions.

Now on to your board's structure. If you're like most boards, you will want to designate different positions, depending on your foundation's culture. For example, most boards have one person leading the foundation—the board chair or president—and other officers such as a vice chair, secretary and treasurer. Some foundation boards use a two-tier structure, where former trustees are elected to serve as honorary members.

Some boards also establish certain standing committees from the start—a nominating committee, for example, that recruits and recommends new members, or a grants committee that reviews proposals. Each committee meets as a small, separate group and reports back to the overall board.

If you are considering changing the size or structure of your board, check with your attorney to see what your organizational documents provide and determine whether it is appropriate to change them.

Board Composition and Member Skills

When it comes to board composition, your choices are many. Some family foundation boards include only immediate family, while others include spouses and extended family. Some automatically award children a place at the board table, while others require the next generation board members to apply for or earn their positions.

Not all family foundation boards are just family. Some invite community members or outside experts to draw upon specific experience or expertise. As many boards find, outside members can bring new ideas and skills to the foundation, as well as community perspective.

Regardless of whether you are an all-family board or have a diverse membership, it's important to set certain membership criteria. It helps to make policy decisions on who is eligible for board service (spouses, for example) before discussing a particular candidate. Your board should identify the skills and qualities you need on the board and develop criteria that will meet your needs. For example, you might look for someone who is enthusiastic about the foundation's mission, who has experience in philanthropy, nonprofit or volunteer work, or who has professional skills or knowledge of one of your funding areas.

Quick Tip

Post your foundation's values, vision and mission statement on the wall of your board meeting room and on top of the board meeting agenda. Refer to these statements often as a group to keep your foundation's larger purpose front and center in every discussion.

Peer Practices

Applying for Board Membership

Many foundations require that new trustees bring some qualifications to the board other than just the family name. The Patrick & Aimee Butler Family Foundation has an application form for potential new board members from third and succeeding generations, which asks about their community activities, work background and areas of interest. "It tells potential trustees that we're serious about our work," said trustee Sandy Butler. "We don't want board members in name only, even if that name is the same as the founder's."

Setting Membership Criteria

"Blood relations may or may not further the mission of a family foundation," said Jaylene Moseley, managing director of the Flintridge Foundation. "The original board of our foundation consisted of the four children of the donor. That first board initially brought on their friends and then recognized that what they needed was to think about criteria."

The Flintridge board formed a nominating committee to oversee the process. Moseley and board members use a written recommendation form to nominate candidates, whether they are family or not. Sometimes they ask grantees for suggestions. Candidates are asked to complete an application, which the nominating committee reviews.

"Anyone in the family is eligible to serve on the board, but we have criteria of what we're looking for in board members," said Moseley. "What's relevant is getting the board members who are most capable in furthering the foundation's mission. We spell out board member responsibilities from the beginning."

Moseley said the foundation's nominating process helped the board focus on the Flintridge mission—instead of family dynamics. "We look at what the foundation needs."

B. Develop bylaws that specify the term length of governing board members; the number of consecutive and/or total terms members may serve; minimum and maximum ages; roles, responsibilities and fiduciary duties; and selection and removal processes.

When your foundation was formed, the original founder(s) or board created bylaws—the internal rules that guide your board's activities. Bylaws typically include a description of the following:

- Board size and structure
- Board membership criteria
- Board selection and removal
- Roles, responsibilities and fiduciary duties
- Terms, term limits and rotation policies
- Minimum and maximum ages of board members
- Attendance policy.

If the above topics aren't already included in your bylaws, you should create policies that address them. Policies, as distinct from bylaws, focus on your foundation's daily operations and practices. Like your bylaws, your policies should be written with your mission and goals in mind.

In Practice Option A, we talked about board size and structure as well as membership. The following discussion will help you craft bylaws or policies for board selection and removal, roles and responsibilities, terms, age limits and attendance.

Note: Your jurisdiction may have specific requirements for what your bylaws should include. Be sure to check with your state's attorney's office for applicable laws relating to bylaws. Remind your board to periodically review the bylaws and amend them as needed.

Board Selection and Removal

Your board should have a process in place to recruit new members so that board openings can be filled or expanded when you decide the time is right. A selection policy will help you respond to family members or prospective trustees who are interested in board membership. When developing a selection policy, it helps to discuss what skills and qualities your board needs in its members and what expertise would help you advance your mission. With these needs in mind, you can write a list describing your membership criteria.

In addition to membership, trustees should also discuss—and state in writing—how the board will handle a situation where a board member must be removed. A policy already in place will give the board objective guidelines to follow at a time that could potentially be unpleasant or awkward. *For sample board selection and removal policies, see the end of this chapter.*

Roles, Responsibilities and Fiduciary Duties

A job description can be a board member's best friend. There's no better tool for describing the board's individual and collective roles and responsibilities. Job descriptions set and differentiate tasks, clarify the relationship between the board and staff (if any) and give board members (and potential members) a clear idea of what they can expect.

Job descriptions can take any written format. Most are one to two pages that include the function, duties and desired characteristics of board members. *For sample job descriptions, see the end of this chapter.*

Term Limits and Rotation Policies

It can be helpful to establish terms, term limits and rotation policies as a way to keep your board fresh and focused. By creating new board openings on a regular basis, your board can bring a continuous flow of new ideas and involvement. If trustees know they only have a finite term of service, they may concentrate their efforts and more attention on foundation activities. Terms and term limits can also make it easier for your board to remove an ineffective trustee, if need be.

Typically, family foundation board members serve two- or three-year terms, with a maximum of two successive terms. Some foundations also limit the total number of years a trustee can serve—typically six years. *For sample term limit and rotation policies, see the end of this chapter.*

Age

Many set a minimum age for board members (typically 21) and a maximum age (typically 75). Setting age limits gives your board a graceful and objective way to select younger board members—and encouraging older members to rotate off.

Attendance

Be sure to include an attendance policy in your bylaws or policies. Some states have guidelines that dictate the minimum number of meetings that trustees must attend (which may be as little as once a year). With new developments in telecommunications, some boards now offer the option to participate in board meetings by conference call or Internet. If your board allows for this kind of participation, put it in writing.

In Their Own Words

Board Job Descriptions Let People Know Their Roles

"When I came to the foundation as executive director in 1999, the board had little clarity on their roles. It was undefined as to who did what. They found it hard to stick to governing the foundation without getting involved in operations. We found we needed more managerial structures in place so that everyone knew what their roles were and what the responsibilities of officers and committees were. This was particularly important with a large board.

"I developed board job descriptions for the separate roles on the board—chair, secretary, treasurer, the executive committee, trustees, etc. The board reviewed the job descriptions, clarified areas of responsibility and approved them. They needed to see something in writing to understand their roles—it became clear to them. Since then, we haven't had to refer much to the actual written position descriptions; the activities and responsibilities have become inculcated as part of the board's culture."

—*Sandra Treacy, executive director, W. Clement & Jessie V. Stone Foundation*

C. Conduct business regularly to ensure meaningful interaction, including at least one annual in-person meeting (governing board and staff, if any).

Meetings bring board members together to do the real "meat and potatoes" work.

Some foundations meet twice yearly, while others meet as often as every other month. Others might meet by phone during the year and hold one annual in-person meeting. Because all other tasks flow from board meetings, the board should plan the annual meeting calendar in advance and distribute materials before each meeting. (See sidebar.)

When determining your board's meeting schedule and location, make choices with respect for board member commitments. For example, if trustees reside in different parts of the country, your board might consider rotating its meeting location. Be sure to schedule meetings far in advance to allow trustees to plan ahead for travel and other arrangements.

Before every board meeting, assign or remind board members of their roles and tasks. Give them all the tools they need to prepare and contribute in a meaningful way.

One of the best tools you can use is a board meeting book. The book includes the agenda, reports and proposal summaries that members should review before the meeting.

The board chair and staff (if any) usually develop the agenda for meetings. A typical foundation meeting agenda includes the following:

- Call to order
- President's report (or administrative report)—announcements, introductions
- Approval of minutes from the previous meeting
- Financial reports—from staff, accountant, board treasurer or the finance committee
- Grant reports—progress reports on current grants, evaluations, annual reports, news
- Grant review—board reviews proposals (or summaries) to determine which ones they will fund and decline
- Unfinished business—a time to discuss any unresolved issues
- New business—new items of consideration
- Outside speakers (as applicable)
- Next meeting—set the schedule
- Adjournment.

Sample Board Meeting Book

A board meeting book might include:

1. Agenda
2. Contact list of board members
3. Previous meeting minutes
4. Financial information
5. Resource development director's report
6. Program director's report
7. Proposal summaries with full proposal attached (if applicable)
8. New business materials
9. Next meeting announcement

In Their Own Words

Scheduling Meetings Can Be a Challenge

"Board members are expected to attend three board meetings a year. This is made clear when we are interviewing board candidates, is stated in the board orientation book they receive and is listed as one of their board responsibilities. Schedules for everyone are normally a challenge. It's challenging to find a day that works for everyone's travel and work schedule. We all work together to settle on the best day possible for everyone.

Recently one of our board members teleconferenced into the meeting. He had an injury that occurred four days prior to the meeting which would not allow for travel. It is stated in our bylaws that 'trustees may participate in any meeting through the use of a conference telephone or similar communications equipment by means of which all persons participating in the meeting can hear each other, and such participation in a meeting shall constitute presence in person at the meeting for all purposes...' As a general rule, we do not teleconference for board meetings, but in this case, we did—and it worked just fine."

—Jean Buckley, president, Tracy Family Foundation

Some family foundations find that an outside facilitator helps in planning and running board meetings. They appreciate having a neutral party at the table and someone who will keep the discussion on topic. The facilitator could be a hired consultant, a family friend or professional associate skilled in facilitation, or a colleague from another foundation.

Remember, the most important tip for meetings: Make sure board members know their roles. The more all participants understand their roles—and the more time they have to prepare for that role—the more productive each meeting will be. "Board meetings are really a function of how well the board works together," said Amy Zell Ellsworth, president of the Zell Family Foundation and senior fellow at The Philanthropic Initative (TPI). "It's so important that everyone is clear about what they're there to do."

D. Stay on mission; all grants are made within grantmaking guidelines. Exceptions are reviewed by the entire board and do not exceed a maximum dollar cap or percentage of total giving.

Your foundation exists for a purpose—your mission. As a part of your charge as a board, you are meant to honor that mission. Your mission should guide every decision you make and every grant you give—it's the key to keeping your foundation's program focused and intact.

As your foundation grows, however, so too may the divergence of your board members' interests. Ideologies may change, commitments may wane and residences might be far, far away from where your foundation funds.

To deal with these challenges, some boards introduce a discretionary grants program.

Discretionary grants are funds distributed at the discretion of one or more board members or in some cases, principal staff. Discretionary grants allow trustees to support organizations that the foundation may not traditionally fund. Others use discretionary grants to fund emergency or interim grants—those that can't wait for the next board meeting.

In the best scenarios, discretionary grants increase board member involvement, incubate new program areas and meet immediate needs. Yet, discretionary grants frequently fall outside the mission and/or geographic focus of the foundation. They may dilute the foundation's mission and create a focus on individual decisions, instead of decisionmaking by the overall board.

By limiting the use of discretionary funds—or keeping them tied to your mission—you can keep your foundation's program strong.

If you do decide to offer discretionary funds, here's a good idea: Decide in advance what type of grantee is permitted. You might develop a discretionary grant request form, for instance, that outlines the requirements. This will make it clear to board members what discretionary grants they can—and cannot—propose. In all cases, the entire board should routinely authorize discretionary grants—before the grants are made. Discretionary grantmaking can raise problems of self-dealing, so proper board vetting and prior approval is the best approach.

In Their Own Words

Sticking to Mission

"The foundation agreed it will only fund what is appropriate for it as a whole. If a trustee wants to expand the grantmaking program to include a new funding area, the board requires that a core group of people are committed to the idea. If there is no leadership or buy-in behind the suggestion, the foundation will not fund it."

—*Kerrie Blevins, foundation director, Patrick & Aimee Butler Family Foundation*

When deciding if a discretionary program is right for your foundation, consider the following questions:

- What would be a reason for funding outside of our mission?

- What do we want to accomplish with discretionary grants?

- Who will be allowed to make discretionary grants?

- How will the board approve discretionary grants?

- What is the maximum discretionary grant amount per person?

- What is the maximum percentage of total grantmaking allowed?

- What requirements must discretionary grants meet (e.g., selection criteria, board reporting requirements)?

If you do allow discretionary grants, remember that the board still holds full fiduciary responsibility over all grants made, and grants must always fall within purposes approved by the IRS.

Peer Practices

Discretionary Grants for Strategic Purposes

The A.L. Mailman Family Foundation in White Plains, NY, sets aside about 10 percent of its budget each year for contributions to affinity groups, professional affiliation fees and officers' discretionary grants. Officers can make small grants to various organizations with which they are connected. These grants don't necessarily need to fit within the foundation's program guidelines—although most all of them do.

"Sometimes we need to make a grant quickly for a strategic purpose. Discretionary grants are a helpful tool for us to do that," said Executive Director and Secretary Luba Lynch. "When a grantee calls with an interesting opportunity for a small grant, we have a flexible way of using our resources to be responsive to the field."

"As of late, though, less of our total grants budget goes to discretionary grants—we would rather keep those dollars within our main program."

E. PROVIDE COMPREHENSIVE ORIENTATION AND TRAINING FOR GOVERNING BOARD MEMBERS.

Orientation is one of those key moments in board members' lives. It introduces them to the foundation—its mission, programs and people—and it acclimates them to the board itself—its structure, operations and legal duties. It's rare for any trustee to "hit the ground running." But you can guide new members along the way, through an orientation that's both effective *and* interesting.

Orientation serves three purposes:

- Clarifies expectations
- Trains members on their legal roles and responsibilities
- Welcomes trustees and makes them feel a part of the board.

Orienting new board members is not a one-time event. It requires that you prepare for the orientation in advance and spend time with new trustees—ideally, over the course of a few orientation sessions or a set period of time.

Think of your foundation as a ship and the board as the crew. You wouldn't feel safe turning over the helm to a crew member who hasn't been trained. The more time you spend with crew members in the beginning, the more confident both they—and you—will feel in their ability to make decisions and contribute in a meaningful way.

How can you be sure that your board receives the best orientation? Here are some tips for creating a solid program.

Agenda

An orientation should always be held as a separate event—a retreat or before a regular board meeting, for example. When it comes to the actual orientation, veteran board members—not the staff—should conduct most of the orientation.

The orientation agenda will vary based on the specific information your board wants to include.

The session might start, for example, with a tour of the foundation's main office (if held on-site) and an introduction of key board members and staff. The board and staff should brief the new members on their roles, and what they like (or find challenging) about working with the foundation.

From there, a typical agenda might include an introduction to the field of philanthropy; an overview of the foundation's history, mission and values, together with a look at its strategic plan and communications; and an explanation of the board's structure and committees. As part of the agenda, plan to go into great detail about the following:

What's expected of board members (for example, terms, attendance, committee work).

A review of finances and grantmaking programs, guidelines and processes.

A discussion of liability and insurance coverage.

An explanation the laws affecting private foundations (self-dealing, for example).

A review and explanation of your foundation's conflict-of-interest policy, code of ethics, reimbursement policy, etc. Some foundations include a site visit or two to grantees as part of orientation, letting the new members see—firsthand—what the foundation's grants have accomplished.

"An orientation shouldn't be a handbook alone."

—Julie Simpson, executive director, Cricket Island Foundation

Board Handbook

Many foundations give new members a board handbook—a "bible" of board history, structure, practices, operations and more. This book introduces them to the board, but also serves as a useful refresher throughout their tenure. Give new members the handbook before their orientation; that way, they will know what to expect and come prepared with questions.

You and the staff (if applicable) should compile materials for the handbook. Consider including the following items:

- **Board directory and calendar**—A roster of board member names, contact and bio information; job descriptions of the chair and members; committee lists; calendar of meetings.
- **Foundation background**—Mission, vision and value statements; history; description of grant-making programs and process; long-range plan; annual report; current grantee list.
- **Board structure**—Terms and term limits; job descriptions for individuals and committees; members' responsibilities and their self-assessment forms.
- **Bylaws and policies**—Articles of incorporation and bylaws; board policies on indemnification and director's and officer's liability insurance; conflict-of-interest policies; code of ethics; attendance policy; compensation and/or expense reimbursements guidelines; document retention and whistle-blower policies.
- **Staff**—Names and job descriptions; personnel policies; organizational chart.
- **Finances**—Investment policy and reports; budget; audit statement; financial procedures; IRS Form 990-PF (or pertinent excerpts).
- **Minutes and issues**—Minutes of recent board meetings; description of current issues for discussion; sample meeting agenda.
- **FAQs**—Frequently asked questions and their answers.
- **Glossary**—A list of philanthropic terms and jargon.

In Their Own Words

Conversation Matters in Orientation

"As a part of our orientation process, our next generation board candidates must attend a minimum of four board meetings in a max of four years, and they must participate on one board committee before they are brought onto the board. They are also required to participate in a series of conversations with members of the family, where older family members can share their knowledge on various nuts and bolts about the foundation—finance, grantmaking, history and more. We want the orientation to be discussion-based. This will teach the new members and, at the same time, encourage relationships among the family."

—Julie Simpson, executive director, Cricket Island Foundation

Outside Training

Some foundations send new board members to outside training or workshops as a part of their orientation. Consider conferences or workshops sponsored by the Council on Foundations, regional associations of grantmakers or affinity groups. You might also consider giving incoming members a subscription to field publications, such as *Foundation News & Commentary*.

Peer Practices

New Board Members Buy In

The Wessell Family Foundation, doing business as The Bright Mountain Foundation in Boulder, Colorado, has held two half-day orientations for its new board members. The first was with the founders, and the second was held when the foundation decided to expand its all-family board to include three community members.

As a part of the orientation, the president, executive director and another board member provided a history of the foundation and its grantmaking activities. "Our biggest goal [for the orientation] was bringing members up to date on what was being funded and how our future looked," said Co-Executive Director Irene Wessell." Afterward, we opened the discussion to what each new member brought to the foundation and examined where they best fit in with our strategic plan."

Wessell believes that her foundation's new board member orientation was successful because she provided information on the foundation, its personnel and programming beforehand. She also encouraged the new board members to open up and talk about themselves. "We wanted them to ask themselves, 'What is my buy-in to the foundation?'" Wessell said. This allowed the orientation program to move toward a more informal, two-way discussion.

F. PROVIDE CONTINUING EDUCATION ON ALL ASPECTS OF FOUNDATION GOVERNANCE, INCLUDING LEGAL, FIDUCIARY AND GRANTMAKING ISSUES.

In addition to giving your board tools and information to help them do a good job, you should encourage them to continue their education on all aspects of foundation management—legal, fiduciary, grantmaking and more. The best way to do this is through professional development opportunities.

Professional development helps members continue their learning and stay motivated. And it doesn't have to be costly or time-consuming. It can be as simple as inviting an outside speaker to a board meeting or sending board members to intensive trainings. Here are some ideas to keep the learning coming:

- **In-house trainings.** Focus on specific subjects such as how to conduct site visits, what to look for in proposals, etc.

- **Outside speakers.** Invite community members, program experts and board development specialists to present at board meetings.

- **Conferences and workshops.** Send new board members to the Council on Foundations' Family Foundations Conference, annual conference or Institute for New Board Members. Check for learning circles, workshops or issues-oriented gatherings offered by regional associations of grantmakers or affinity groups.

- **Periodical subscriptions.** Give incoming members subscriptions to publications such as the Council on Foundations' magazine *Foundation News & Commentary*, or the *Chronicle of Philanthropy*.

- **Articles and policy papers.** Share publications to prompt discussion and keep members abreast of new developments in the field.

- **Leadership opportunities.** Encourage board members to volunteer on a Council on Foundations committee to share leadership with the field.

When considering professional development, ask board members what kind of activities interest them. Find ways for the board to connect with the members of the community, through site visits or events, for example—or their peers, at conferences and workshops. Inform your board about upcoming events in the field. Check with the Council on Foundations (www.cof.org) for a schedule.

Sample Board Rotation Policy

The Board of Directors shall consist of seven (7) members. Five (5) of these will be family, defined as direct descendants of the Foundation's original donor. Three (3) of these will be the children and two (2) will be the grandchildren of the donor. The grandchildren will serve 2-year terms on a rotating basis. Two (2) of the Board members will be from the community, not direct descendants of the donor, and will serve a maximum of two consecutive 3-year terms.

The rotation of grandchildren serving on the board is determined by age beginning with the oldest grandchild. Each grandchild must be 21 before he or she is elected to the Board. Minor children will enter the rotation on their 21st birthday.

Sample Board Removal Policy

Courtesy of the John Gogian Family Foundation

Section 3.09. Removal. The Board may declare vacant the office of a director who has been declared of unsound mind by a final order of court, or convicted of a felony, or found by a final order of judgement of any court to have breached any duty arising under Chapter 2, Article 3 of the California Nonprofit Public Benefit Corporation Law. The Board, by affirmative vote of a majority of the Directors then in office, may remove any Director without cause.

Sample Board Member Job Description

Courtesy of The Leighty Foundation

Board Members:

- Determine, articulate and support the purpose and mission of the Foundation
- Elect the Board and determine the bylaws of the Foundation
- Attend the meetings of the Board by conference call or in person
- Assure that the Foundation functions within appropriate legal and fiscal constraints
- Research funding opportunities in areas of interest of the Foundation
- Initiate relationships with potential grantees
- Serve as advocate for the cause of potential grantees
- Conduct site visits
- Participate in grant follow ups and evaluations (if not a staff function)
- Build relationships and collaborate with other funders
- Review investment philosophy and investment opportunities for the Foundation
- Engage in lifelong learning in areas of interest and expertise
- Serve as catalysts for information sharing
- Assist each other as requested

Sample Letter Inviting an Individual to Apply for a Board Position

Courtesy of the Flintridge Foundation

Dear (name):

I am pleased to write this letter, letting you know that you have been recommended as a candidate to serve on the Flintridge Foundation's Board of Directors.

This letter and our web site (www.FlintridgeFoundation.org) are offered as an overview of the Flintridge Foundation, its activities and personnel. I have also enclosed an Application in the hope that you are interested in applying for a position on our board.

This is a family foundation that has operated since 1985. The Foundation was created and funded by Francis and Louisa Moseley. Since that time, our board's composition has changed and currently includes one of the donors' children, two adult grandchildren and four non-family members.

In 2003, the Foundation provided technical assistance and grants totaling over $1 million. We are narrowly focused in the following program areas: (1) Conservation: fish, forestry and riparian projects in the Pacific Northwest; (2) Theatre Arts: ensemble theatres employing a collaborative creative process; (3) Visual Arts: individual artist awards; (4) Community Services: fundraising and other technical assistance for community-based organizations in Pasadena and Altadena that serve children and youth.

The Board meets during three or four weekends each year, typically on Friday and Saturday. Our meetings include reviewing and discussing grant proposals, awarding grants, and monitoring financial operations; in addition, the staff often includes supplementary presentations and information to keep the board well informed in the Foundation's funding fields of interest.

The responsibilities of our Board Members include thoroughly reading the docket before each meeting, being available for up to four site visits with staff each year, and participating in Board and Committee discussions and decisions.

Our board members do not receive compensation. However, the Foundation does reimburse members for all travel expenses. We strongly believe in our responsibility as stewards. As a consequence, we strictly avoid even the appearance of conflicts-of-interest; we do not mix our personal giving with the Foundation's work; we adhere to processes of communications and grant review that have been carefully developed to provide clear and objective information and access for nonprofit organizations working in our fields of interest.

This Application is for a three-year term, 2004 through 2006. If you decide that being a board member is a commitment you would like to make, we would be delighted to hear from you. Please complete and return the Application within the next two weeks, and we will include it with other applications in the board's meeting docket. The board will only be selecting one new board member at this time. If you have questions or need clarification, please call our Managing Director, _____ at 555/555-5555.

Sample Trustee Application Form

Courtesy of the Patrick & Aimee Butler Family Foundation

NAME _____ DATE _____

ADDRESS _____

TELEPHONE (O) _____ (H) _____

BIRTHDATE _____ EMAIL _____

EDUCATIONAL BACKGROUND:

INSTITUTION _____ YEAR _____

DEGREE/MAJOR _____

INSTITUTION _____ YEAR _____

DEGREE/MAJOR _____

OCCUPATION _____

Please check your areas of greatest expertise based on educational or professional, volunteer or personal experience:

_____ Finance	_____ Fundraising
_____ Investments	_____ Critical Analysis
_____ Planning/Public Policy	_____ Legal Affairs
_____ Public Relations/Marketing	_____ Other

Please check the Foundation program areas in which you are interested:

ARTS & HUMANITIES

_____ Historical Societies

_____ Humanities

_____ Museums

_____ Theatre

ENVIRONMENT

_____ Water Quality Issues

_____ Land Use & Preservation

_____ Environmental Education

HUMAN SERVICE

_____ Abuse

_____ Chemical Dependency

_____ Housing

_____ Children, Youth & Families

PHILANTHROPY & CIVIC AFFAIRS

_____ Non-profit Assistance

_____ Civic Affairs

List current or past membership on non-profit or community boards of directors:

Sample Board Candidate Interview Questions

Courtesy of the Lydia B. Stokes Foundation

- What has been important to you in your life?

- What are your most important life values/principles?

- What organizations have you supported with donations and/or time?

- What causes are important to you?

- What principles are important to you in your business life? How do you conduct your business life?

- How are you involved in your community?

- How do you participate in charitable giving?

- What gifts/talents can you bring to this foundation?

- Do you see yourself having adequate time for this work?

- Would you be interested in spending time finding out about organizations in your area to support? Would you be willing to do site visits and follow ups?

- Would you be able to attend the annual meeting each year?

- How do you feel about joining a board that has been small and very close in its sense of family and commitment to principles?

- How do you feel about being part of an extended family group?

- Have you had much experience with, or have you been interested in, philanthropic activities? If so, what are they?

- What does philanthropy mean to you?

- What is your philosophy regarding socially responsible investing? Do you utilize guidelines in your own investment choices?

- Are you acquainted with Quaker philosophy and peace work?

- Do you have any questions regarding our mission statement? Do you agree with its philosophy?

Sample New Board Member Interview

Courtesy of the Flintridge Foundation

INTERVIEW AGENDA

Applicant:_____(name)_____

Date: _____   Time: _____

1. *Introductions:* each committee member, then the applicant.

2. *President:* description of the work the Foundation is doing; cover the Foundation's support of grassroots efforts and groups that represent diverse cultures.

3. *Committee Chair:* description of responsibilities of board members.

Questions (alternate among committee members):

   a. What would you like us to know about you?

       Why do you think it would be interesting to be a part of the Foundation's work?

       What role do you think community organizations play in society?

       Are you comfortable with the Foundation's established programs, which involve controversial art, diverse cultures and grassroots efforts? Will these established programs be a good fit for your expertise, skills and interests?

       What do you consider to be the most important characteristics and values of a foundation board member?

   f. Are you comfortable with the board member responsibilities and time commitments outlined by the Chair?

   g. What has been one of your most interesting work or philanthropic experiences?

   h. Other questions that the committee members may wish to ask.

Chair: call for final questions (both of committee members and applicant).

Concluding remarks.

Sample Board Member Orientation Process

Courtesy of the Lydia B. Stokes Foundation

Orientation/Mentoring Process:

- Family and foundation history.
- Legal requirements of the foundation.
- Administration and organizational structure.
- Areas of giving and specific grants.

New trustee receives packet containing:

- Mission statement
- Grantee guidelines
- List of grants for past 3 years
- Investment policy SRI guidelines
- Copy of chapter in Legacy book
- Pratt video-show at annual meeting
- Stories/transcripts of Grandmother and family
- Legal aspects of foundations and trustee responsibilities
- Council on Foundations' Stewardship Principles for Family Foundations
- Materials on grant writing
- Pertinent publications, books

YEAR ONE

Term begins at annual meeting.

Transition ceremony.

Show Pratt video, stories of Legacy and family, Q&A during annual meeting.

First Fall—New Trustee:

- Is included in fall conference call.
- Fall grants to be sent ahead of time to new Trustee.
- Attends Council on Foundations offerings, Regional Association of Grantmakers conference or Council on Foundations Family Foundations Conference during the first year.

First Spring—New Trustee:

- Works with other Trustees to make grants.
- Goal of first year is for new Trustee to get an understanding and feel for the Foundation.
- What makes the LBS Foundation unique? What are we all about?

YEAR TWO

New Trustee begins own grant making

Sample Meeting Minutes

Present:

Guests in Attendance:

Excused Absences:

Absent:

I. **Call to Order**—The meeting was called to order at 9:00 a.m. by Chair.

II. **Opening Remarks from the Chair**—Chair Robert WHEELER welcomed new board members, Jane SMITH and John BROWN.

III. **Approval of Consent Agenda**—James JONES moved that the consent agenda be approved. Kate LEE seconded the motion.

IV. **Financial Report**—Accountant Bob SMITH reported on grants paid since the period ending September 2001, and the distributable amount for the upcoming quarter.

V. **Foundation Administrator's Report**—Beverly JONES reported on current grant programs and new proposals submitted.

VI. **Proposal Review and Allocation**—Board members broke into teams of three to review and present proposals. The board voted to approve the following three grants for the upcoming quarter.

Children's Health Services—$25,000

Family Center of Chester County—$50,000

The Hope Shelter—$25,000

VII. **New Business**—Kate LEE announced the upcoming Council on Foundations Family Foundation conference and asked which board members will attend. The board voted to send Kate LEE, Beverly JONES and Jane SMITH to the conference.

VIII. **Adjournment**—Chair Robert WHEELER announced that the next meeting will be held on October 17 and adjourned the meeting.

CHAPTER 3
Giving Means More Than Making Grants

PRINCIPLE III:

WE CONSIDER MULTIPLE STRATEGIES TO FURTHER OUR MISSION.

Grantmaking is at the heart of your family foundation's work. In essence, it's why you do what you do. It shows your commitment to make a difference in the community and the way you fulfill that commitment.

Chapter 2 discussed the role of the board in furthering the foundation's mission. Yet, there's more to meeting your foundation's mission than making grants. While grantmaking always is the primary philanthropic vehicle for foundations, there are other, equally worthwhile, strategies.

These strategies are often referred to as direct charitable activities—activities tied to your mission, but that go beyond grantmaking. Examples include collaborations, convenings, evaluating grants, mission-related investing and more.

In this chapter, you'll go deeper into defining and strengthening your overall grantmaking program. Here, you'll find practice options that take your program to the next level—allowing you to be a true *learning organization*. You'll discover how to use best practice models and learn from your peers. You'll learn why professional development and personal giving help board members and staff stay enthused and engaged. And you'll learn how advocacy work can make changes that last.

Stop for a moment here and ask yourself and your board: *What is it that we most want to accomplish? What tools would help us get there?* This chapter will show you the many options available.

IN THIS CHAPTER

- Decide which grant types work best for you
- Evaluate grants
- Collaborate with and convene other foundations and nonprofits
- Promote personal giving by foundation board and staff
- Conduct mission-related investing
- Fund and engage in public policy advocacy work.

PRACTICE OPTIONS FOR PRINCIPLE III

A. LEARN BEST PRACTICE MODELS AND COMPARE PRACTICES AGAINST OTHERS IN THE FIELD.

Good news. By reading this book, you are practicing the very Practice Option described here. But there's a catch. It takes more than just reading. As one family foundation trustee said, "Practice models are great, but they don't do anything for us if we are *only* reading them."

For practice models to work, you have to take them back to your board, actively discuss them and compare them against your own practices. This will help you celebrate what you're doing well and improve on areas where you could do better.

There are countless practice models available in the field—not only in this book, but also in many others. Do you have a particular area where your foundation could use some help? Here are some ideas on where you can learn more:

- Talk to your colleagues to see what they have done. Ask them if they have any sample documents and tailor those samples to your own needs.
- Attend conferences and workshops to stay on top of best practices.
- Network with your foundation colleagues at local, regional or national events.
- Subscribe to publications about family foundations or the field of philanthropy.
- Visit the Council's website, as well as the websites of your colleagues. Note particularly the sample documents and interviews at http://bestpractices.cof.org/family.
- Contact the Council's Family Foundation Services department (family@cof.org) for assistance.

For more information on finding best practices, read "Scanning the Environment for Philanthropic Best Practice Systems," by Thomas E. Backer and John Bare, *Foundation News & Commentary,* November/December 1999. Visit www.foundationnews.org.

In Their Own Words

Sample Documents Can Spark Ideas

"When developing board descriptions for different trustee roles, I found it helpful to look at other foundation's sample documents. I found many of these through the Council on Foundations and the Association of Small Foundations. I was able to get ideas from these sample documents and tailored them to meet our specific needs."

—*Sandra Treacy, executive director, W. Clement & Jessie V. Stone Foundation*

B. Consider a range of financial support options that could include: general operating, project, capital, research, scholarship, endowment, multiyear and challenge grants, and funds to respond to emergency or other unanticipated needs.

Few, if any, of your activities will be as visible as the grants that you make. Your foundation should take the time to thoroughly define—and constantly redefine—its grantmaking. In doing so, you might consider a range of financial support options.

As you'll read below, there are many types of grants, some of which serve a different purpose. Some of them may or may not be right for you, depending on your mission, capacity and program goals. If you are a foundation just starting up, the first step in defining your grantmaking program is always to ask yourselves this: *What do we want to accomplish? What grantmaking tools will help us achieve our goal?*

In other words, don't put the egg before the chicken. Don't decide that you want to do a challenge grant, just for the sake of doing a challenge grant. Look first at what you want to achieve by way of your mission and goals and then examine your options to see which type of grant would best serve you.

Let's take a look at those options. Even if you are an established foundation, reviewing the options below will remind you of your choices and make sure your grantmaking is still accomplishing your goals, given our changing society.

Grants are generally categorized according to the purpose they serve for the grantee.

- **Program/project grants** support programmatic activities of a grantee to achieve a defined projected outcome, whereas **general support grants** (also called **unrestricted or operating**) support an organization's overall activities including operating expenses and overhead. General grants may be used at the discretion of the grantee.

- **Capital grants** support "bricks and mortar" projects such as purchasing land, constructing facilities or undertaking similar activities.

- **Research or planning grants** give organizations and/or individuals the time, support and leverage to plan ahead and gather information for a specific project.

- **Start up, also called seed grants,** offer funds for new programs or organizations. The grantee can use the funds for planning, feasibility studies or the initial costs of staff and operation. **Demonstration grants** are a type of seed grant that may serve as a model for replication in the future.

- **Capacity-building grants** (also sometimes called **technical assistance**) offer operational or management assistance to a nonprofit, for example, by paying for the services of a consultant to help improve the organization's ability to serve its purpose. This type of grantmaking can also be applied to a systemic change in a field.

- **Scholarships** are grants to individuals (or to an institution, who will then make the grant to a student), usually for educational or research purposes.

Other grants are not characterized by how the grantee will use them, but according to a certain condition. For example:

- **Matching or challenge grants** are given on the condition that the grantee raise additional funds (often the same amount, but sometimes more or less) from other donors for the same purpose. These grants help leverage a larger grant than the foundation could alone provide.

- **Contingency grants** also depend on a stipulation—hiring a financial officer, for example, or reforming a practice. A foundation can often encourage better practices among its grantees with these grants.

- **Endowments** stipulate that the grantee does not spend the principal but can use income from the grant to meet general operating expenses or for uses specified by the foundation. An endowment grant consists of cash, stock or virtually any other asset.

Still, other grants can be categorized by when or how they are paid or by a certain grantmaking strategy:

- **Interim grants** can be approved by the board or staff to address immediate needs that can't wait for the next board meeting. Sometimes interim grants are known as **emergency grants**, if they are in response to a natural disaster or other kind of crisis.

- **Multiyear grants** are those paid incrementally over a period of time. These can lend stability to organizations and maximize the return on the foundation's investment. They may also obligate a foundation's funds into the future.

- **Leveraged grants** occur when an amount of money is given with the express purpose of attracting funding from other sources or of providing the organization with the tools it needs to raise other kinds of funds. This is sometimes called the "multiplier effect." A foundation might help a grantee by suggesting other funders, making calls on the grantee's behalf or collaborating with other grantmakers.

Not every family foundation offers the grants listed here. Foundations often customize their grants to suit their own program or community circumstances.

Peer Practices

Building Capacity in Grantees

The Richard & Susan Smith Family Foundation wanted to enable capable, well-led nonprofits to do substantially more of what they were already doing well.

Executive Director David Ford met with leaders of Boston's major foundations and asked them which were the best-functioning and best-led organizations in the area. He then invited several recommended nonprofits to compete for multiyear capacity-building grants to build their infrastructure. The grants would be awarded over five years, and total about 10 percent of the nonprofits' operating budgets. Nine grants were awarded.

"So far, the nine grantees are growing at an average of about 25 to 30 percent per year," said Ford. "For each grantee, we negotiate benchmarks each year for their growth and the quality of services they provide. Grantees must meet these benchmarks, or renegotiate, in order to receive the next year's contribution."

C. Use program and grant evaluation to improve outcomes.

As part of good grantmaking, you monitor grants throughout the grant cycle, through site visits, grant reports or other methods. This helps you make sure the grant money is spent the way it's supposed to be. Grant monitoring involves the grantee setting goals and reporting to the foundation on the degree of success or failure along the way.

Although similar in nature, grant evaluation is very different from grant monitoring. Evaluation describes an overall assessment that shows *what has changed* because of the grant or, to a larger degree, the grantmaking program. In addition to grant monitoring, your foundation should use program and grant evaluation to improve your outcomes.

When you evaluate a grant program, you take an in-depth look at the results and accomplishments of your grants. Evaluation helps your foundation:

- Be accountable to the public
- Improve your grantmaking, now and in the future
- Assess the quality or impact of funded programs
- Plan and implement new programs
- Increase your knowledge of the community and organizations
- Inform future grant decisions
- Bring more credibility to your work.

Evaluation also helps your grantees in many ways, including to:

- Articulate their progress
- Improve their work
- Demonstrate their accountability.

Your board should establish a policy on how and when your foundation will conduct its evaluations and who will be responsible for the task—for example, the staff, a board member or committee, or an outside evaluator.

Keep in mind there are many ways to evaluate. Some foundations—especially smaller foundations—shy away from evaluation, thinking it an insurmountable task. "Who has the time?" they wonder. But there are many simple ways to evaluate, suitable for foundations of any size, such as:

- Grantee self-evaluation
- Site visit by trustees
- Hiring an outside evaluator experienced in evaluation
- Asking a college or graduate student at a local university
- Engaging the help of a foundation intern or next generation family member.

Remember, too, that not all of your grants require the same level of evaluation. Your criteria can—and will—vary from grant to grant. You might only evaluate grantees that received above a certain dollar amount, for example.

The key is to define (or have the grantee define) upfront what determines "success" for a particular grant or initiative. In other words, determine the evaluation criteria in advance of making a grant, ideally before the grant is first awarded.

For some grants, you might look at quantitative data, such as how many people were served and why that made a difference. With others, you might examine the qualitative results of the grant, answering questions such as "How do clients feel about their circumstances as a result of the grant?" In any case, criteria should relate to the grant or program purpose and should be defined at the onset of the grant.

When developing an evaluation process, consider these questions:

- What do we want to know in a year from now that you don't know today?
- What are the three most important things to learn from this grant/initiative?
- What success stories have come from the grant(s)?
- How should we receive evaluation results?
- How will we use the information from the evaluation?
- How can we gain feedback on the granting process from grantees?

No matter how you evaluate your grants or programs, a good rule is keep it simple. Collecting data takes times and work. The fewer questions you ask grantees, the more efficient they will be in giving you answers.

Some excerpts above adapted from "Seven Reasons to Evaluate," Foundation News & Commentary, January/February 1993. Visit www.foundationnews.org.

D. Share successes, failures and lessons learned from grant and program evaluations internally and externally as appropriate.

Learn something? Share it. It's as simple as that.

Earlier we talked about going beyond your grantmaking to become a full-fledged *learning organization*. A learning organization is just that—an organization that is committed to continual learning.

But what does that mean, exactly? Let's take a look.

To become a learning organization, you constantly question the future. You evaluate where you have been and demonstrate what you've learned. You share your successes—and, more importantly, your failures.

You read. You talk. You listen.

You understand—even though you might be sitting alone in an office all day—that you do not work in isolation. You are part of something bigger than yourself, your family, your board and your grantees—you are part of a field and *you* have something to offer.

At times in the field of family foundations, people are hesitant to speak up—to share what it is they do and why. No one thinks they're an expert. The truth is, everyone's an expert in their own way. Because family foundations are as different as the families they represent, there is always something to learn.

If your foundation conducts an evaluation of a grant or program, get the word out. Let your colleagues know what you did—what worked and what you might do differently.

Be sure the board and staff review and discuss the results and use them as a part of your future planning. Post the results on your website, if you have one, or as a part of your communications to the family or field. Publish what you've learned in a field publication—such as the Council's *Family Matters* or *Foundation News & Commentary*, or one of your regional association newsletters or bulletins. Submit a practice to the COF principles database for family foundations at http://bestpractices.cof.org/family.

When you share with others, you learn from others. That's what being a learning organization is all about.

To learn more about sharing lessons learned, read "That Was a Clunker," by Roger M. Williams, Foundation News & Commentary, *July/August 1999. Visit www.foundationnews.org.*

E. Collaborate with others who fund similar work.

Your foundation alone cannot solve every community issue or problem. At a time when resources are limited and social issues are complex, more and more foundations see the value in collaborating.

A collaboration is a well-defined, mutually beneficial relationship you enter into with one or more organizations to achieve a common goal. By working with others in the community, you can best use your available resources and provide another opportunity to learn from your colleagues. Collaborations can create new energy and ideas, and usually result in increased resources.

There are other benefits as well. Collaborations bring buy-in from many sectors in the community. When groups and organizations play a role in the decisionmaking on an issue, they are more likely to involve themselves in the work to be done.

Second, collaborations open channels of communication. Many times, different groups are working on the same issue, sometimes without even knowing it. Collaboration centralizes their effort, and avoids duplicating the work others have done.

Third, collaborations allow input from diverse voices in the community (racial, cultural, socioeconomic) that otherwise might not be heard. This can create a richer and more lasting response to problem solving.

So how do you start collaborating? There's more than one way to do it, and your strategies will vary, depending on the issue or task at hand.

In any collaboration, consider the following steps:

- Ask yourselves: *What do we want to change or accomplish? Who might help us reach our goals?*
- Identify and approach potential partners.
- Take time to understand the vision and mission of those partners.
- Collectively define the goals, actions and outcomes of the collaboration, so all parties are clear and committed to the plan.
- Carefully develop agreements with all partners to the collaboration, outlining duties and expectations for the work.
- Design an exit strategy so that each organization knows when it has fulfilled its obligation.

One type of collaboration is a joint funding project. Sometimes a foundation joins other grantmakers to support a project of common interest—usually in situations where no single funder has the resources to support it completely. Joint funding projects can be a good way to leverage funds *and* time.

Keep in mind: Collaborations are hard work. Whenever you work with other organizations or people, you might encounter challenges, such as organizational and/or personal egos, one group taking too much credit for the work, misunderstandings or unexpected twists and turns. In most cases, if all parties communicate clearly and gain a mutual understanding of what is expected, you can avoid potential pitfalls.

The benefits of collaborating, however, usually outweigh any challenges. Collaborations create a valuable forum, where community partners can come together for the greater good. That might sound like a cliché. Yet, when funders bring their collective expertise and perspective to an issue, they are more likely to burst forth with big ideas.

Peer Practices

Collaborations Extend Your Reach

The Lois & Richard England Family Foundation has been involved in several collaborative funding initiatives in Washington, DC. Years ago, the foundation joined the Public Education Reform Partnership, whose members included funders; the public school system; and DC Agenda, a nonprofit dedicated to public education reform. The foundation became involved as a means of addressing a social policy question of concern to the foundation's trustees. According to director Margie Siegel, "Giving time as well as funding to such initiatives is an excellent way for a smaller family foundation to gain visibility and extend its reach. At the time, the partnership opened exciting new opportunities and created new access for us in a funding area in which we wanted to be an active player."

F. ENSURE THAT STAFF (IF ANY) IS WELL-QUALIFIED AND RECEIVES ONGOING PROFESSIONAL DEVELOPMENT.

If there's one thing foundations have learned, it's this: The more skilled their staff and board, the better their organizations will be. If you have a staff, you will want to keep them well-qualified for the job. Ongoing professional development is one way to do this.

Professional development helps your staff improve their knowledge and skills. Many activities fall under the category "professional development," such as attending Council on Foundations' conferences or other regional workshops; conducting in-house trainings; networking with peers, subscribing to field publications and more.

When family foundations offer professional development opportunities, they show a commitment to their staff—one that both motivates and rewards. Staff will be much happier and more productive as they continually learn and grow professionally. With training and education, they can stay abreast of developments in the field—and bring that learning back to the board.

When considering professional development activities, you might start by asking employees: *What motivates you? What do you like most/least about what you do? What would make working here more rewarding for you?*

Recognizing the importance of professional development, some family foundations include it as a line item in their administrative budget. They might allocate a set dollar amount for each staff member or designate it as one lump sum.

If your board questions the value of professional development, remind them that a well-trained staff ensures the foundation's interests are well represented in the community. How well your staff communicates is crucial to protecting and promoting the foundation's good name and good work.

"If you're interested in professional development, there's all kinds of information out there—regional grantmaking associations, funders' forums, affinity groups, conferences, meetings with other foundation program officers. All you have to do is look, and you'll find an opportunity to learn."

—Kathleen Odne, executive director, Dean & Margaret Lesher Foundation

G. PROMOTE FOUNDATION BOARD AND STAFF PERSONAL GIVING AND VOLUNTEERISM (BEARING IN MIND POTENTIAL CONFLICTS OF INTEREST).

Foundation work builds a culture of philanthropy—one that often extends outside the boardroom and into the homes, families and hearts of the people doing the work.

Many find it rewarding to practice their own form of philanthropy or volunteer work. When you encourage your board and staff members to seek giving opportunities *outside* the foundation, you may find they become even more engaged *in* the foundation.

To encourage personal giving among staff, a foundation might create a matching gifts program. The Clowes Fund, for example, created a program which matches employees charitable gifts up to $1,000 per calendar year to any qualified charitable organization that is within the foundation's grantmaking interests. The Clowes Fund budgets $4,000 annually for this program to match gifts. "Staff members are delighted to be able to leverage additional gifts for their favorite causes," said Executive Director Beth Casselman.

"We see philanthropy not only in terms of the dollars, but in donating our time to nonprofits as well."

—Luba Lynch, A.L. Mailman Family Foundation

"You might also offer staff time off to volunteer for their favorite charitable organization. For example, at the Dyson Foundation, each full-time staff member receives one week paid leave per year to volunteer for a nonprofit organization of his or her choosing. Whenever staff goes on volunteer leave, they are asked to present and discuss their experience at the next staff meeting. According to executive vice president Diana Gurieva, "Not only is this good for our staff—both in terms of morale and their understanding of voluntary organizations—but outsiders also see this as proof positive of our real commitment to our community."

In Their Own Words

Volunteering to Help Grantees

"We support our largest grantee, Mission Honduras, financially through grants, but do other things to help them as well. A few years ago, the three U.S.-based volunteers for the mission left about the same time. It was up to us to step up to help the program. We found a manager for the program—the first paid staff person in the U.S.— and I took on the volunteer training. I coordinate scheduling and information for their very active volunteer program (About 400 people—mostly church and school groups—make the trip there annually.).

"We also help the mission fundraise through grantwriting and appeals at local churches. We helped them put together an annual fundraising video presentation, and a couple of years ago, even organized a charitable event for their benefit—a square dance held at a local campground."

—*Tom Teeling, board secretary and executive director, John & Susan Dewan Foundation*

H. PROVIDE TECHNICAL ASSISTANCE TO GRANTEES AND OTHER NONPROFITS.

Sometimes grantees and other philanthropic organizations need more than funding—they need a little technical know-how.

Technical assistance is a broad term that can fall under many other names: capacity building, organizational development, funding infrastructure, increasing sustainability.

All of these describe activities that strengthen an organization from the inside out, so that it may better fulfill its mission.

Technical assistance takes many forms, including grantmaking or nongrantmaking activities. It can be offered directly by a foundation or can be in the form of a grant to pay for the services of an outside consultant. For example, a foundation might offer:

- **Fundraising assistance**—helping nonprofits write better grants; suggesting other grantmakers; calling other funders on behalf of the nonprofit.

- **Public relations**—helping grantees promote their grants and their programs; providing them with press release and press kit samples; training their staff in how to work with the media.

- **Budgeting and financial planning**—hiring a consultant to help with accounting.

- **Program planning or evaluation**—conducting a formal evaluation of the organization's effectiveness; hiring a facilitator for strategic planning.

- **Professional development**—sending staff to conferences, workshops or leadership courses; paying for subscriptions or membership fees; hiring an outside consultant to conduct an in-house training session or board or staff retreat.

- **New equipment or technology**—purchasing new computers, software, office equipment, materials.

- **Marketing**—paying for the writing, design or printing of brochures, educational materials or an annual report; paying for staff to attend marketing courses.

- **General operating grants**—combining one or more of the above.

Many foundations believe that technical assistance benefits nonprofits more than project funding. By providing *expertise* or *equipment* in addition to grant dollars, you can help your nonprofit partners function better over time.

Of course, providing technical assistance isn't right for every foundation. Some foundations feel that technical assistance borders on being meddlesome with grantees. Plus it can be challenging—and the work is neverending. Because it's not as results-oriented as a project grant might be, it can also be tough to keep your foundation board members interested.

No one knows this more than the Mary Reynolds Babcock Foundation, which has been offering support for organizational development to grantees since 1995. "The reality is that organizational development grants are boring compared to program grants. They all look alike." said executive director Gayle Williams. To keep the board enthusiastic about its work, the board members personally connect with grantees.

"Our board members do a site visit once a year, and we sometimes invite grantees to present at board meetings. They talk about what a difference organizational development makes to them and to the community."

*"Our foundation wants to be more than check writers—
we want to get involved in helping our grantees."*

—Tom Teeling, John & Susan Dewan Foundation

In spite of its challenges, the payoff for offering support for organizational capacity building is clear. "We see the impact of how these grants translate into stronger organizations and stronger communities," said Williams.

When considering whether giving technical assistance is right for you, ask yourselves these questions:

- What is more important to us—investing in new projects or building an organization's capacity over time?

- In what kinds of technical assistance would we be willing and eager to invest?

- If we decide to give technical assistance, what criteria would an organization have to meet before it would be eligible?

- How would we work with nonprofits to determine their needs and readiness for technical assistance?

- How engaged should we be when working with nonprofits? How close is too close?

- How long would we need to see the results of our technical assistance efforts? Are we willing to wait that long?

For more information on technical assistance, read "Capacity Building Strategies," Family Matters, *Spring 2002. Visit www.cof.org.*

In Their Own Words

Footing the Bill for Consultants

"At the Dale & Edna Walsh Foundation, we work with smaller organizations, including some grassroots operations. We've found that a lot of organizations have great missions and great people, but they don't always have the business skills they need. If we see how they might improve on a certain skill, prior to giving them a grant we will often pay a consultant to teach them how to market themselves, how to improve their image, how to fundraise, how to prepare and analyze their business plan, how to manage their finances—whatever their organizational needs might be.

"To determine their needs, we go on a site visit and ask them questions. For example, I may visit a small nonprofit looking for money to print brochures and see that its current literature needs redesigning. I would tell them, 'We want to help you; we want to give you money. But first, let us pay someone to create a better brochure for you—or teach you how to create a better one yourself. Then, we'll give you the money to print them. It is a simple way for us to help them and feel better about spending the foundation's dollars."

—*Shai Edberg, executive director and trustee, Dale & Edna Walsh Foundation*

Excerpt from Family Matters, *Spring 2002. Visit www.cof.org*

I.

INVEST IN WAYS THAT FURTHER THE MISSION (E.G., PROGRAM-RELATED INVESTMENTS, MICROCREDIT LOANS, SOCIALLY RESPONSIBLE INVESTING, AND PROXY/VOTING/SHAREHOLDER RESOLUTIONS).

Ready to take your program to the next level? Look for ways outside of grants and technical assistance to fulfill your mission—look to your own investments.

There are many ways to support your mission through your own investments. For example, many foundations make loans or microcredit loans to nonprofits or other entities, often at below-market rates or no interest. Some foundations offer a loan guarantee to organizations (also called fiscal sponsorship), reinsuring commercial loans extended by banks. Others tailor their investment portfolio to match their foundation's mission—called socially responsible investing. And finally, some foundations participate in active proxy voting and shareholder resolutions.

Program-related Investments

A program-related investment (PRI) is an investment made by a foundation to accomplish a charitable objective related to its mission. This type of investment is a good way to support grantees as they become more self-sufficient.

A PRI's purpose isn't to produce income, obtain capital appreciation or otherwise make money for the foundation. In fact, many loans are set at zero or below-market interest rates. According to the IRS, there are two characteristics that distinguish PRIs from traditional foundation investments: (1) a charitable purpose is the primary motivation and (2) generating income is *not* a significant motivation. To ensure that it meets those requirements, a foundation should document the investment's purpose when it makes the PRI.

Program-related investments may take many forms, including loans, loan guarantees, real estate mortgages, stock purchases and other investments that offer both *financial* and *programmatic* returns.

The amount of the loan qualifies as satisfying your minimum distributions requirement (payout) for that year. When the loan is repaid, however, the amount must be added back into the assets upon which payout is calculated. (*See chapter 4 for more on payout.*)

Like any investment, PRIs are not without risk. Yet, the return on that risk can be worth it. Always consult your attorney or accountant before making this type of investment. For more information, refer to the Council's *Program-Related Investment Primer,* 1993, or "Current Practices in Program-Related Investing," *NFG Reports: Newsletter of the Neighborhood Funders Group,* Fall 2004, www.nfg.org.

In Their Own Words

Loan Guarantees

"For years, we've offered a loan guarantee program to nonprofits. We consider it a program-related investment because we help them build their capacity with a below-interest loan. Our guarantee allows the bank to loan to them at a reasonable rate. It's been a challenging program because the banks don't like to take on high risk loans. As a result, we're exploring new ways to fund loans."

—*Susan Halliday, director of finance, Jacobs Family Foundation*

Peer Practices

Filling in the Gaps

When the Helen Bader Foundation sought to increase the leverage of its four local program areas in 2001, it created a $5 million fund dedicated to various non-grant investments—loans, loan guarantees, program-related investments and equity investments—that could bolster nonprofit and for-profit projects aligned with the foundation's mission. "Our primary objective isn't to make money, but to help fill gaps in the community," said vice president Lisa Hiller. One of our top criteria is that our participation strengthens the deal, as many of these projects are risky and do not easily attract mainstream financing sources."

Hiller cautioned that there are significant legal costs in starting a PRI program, and you can't use regular grant evaluations. "When you're making term loans, the programmatic returns can be huge, but keep in mind that the risk can be equally significant," she said.

Microcredit Loans

Microcredit is the practice of extending small loans to people in impoverished nations. These loans help them generate self-employment projects to improve their standard of living. This method of loaning is also called microfinance, microlending, peer lending and village banking.

In a microcredit setting, a funder makes a small loan, typically $50 to $200, to a person or small group, allowing them to meet their basic needs and become economically self-sufficient. For example, a woman may borrow $50 to buy chickens so she can sell eggs. As the chickens multiply, she will have more eggs to sell. Soon she can sell the chicks. Each expansion pulls her further away from poverty.

Unlike other loan programs, microfinance does not require clients to have collateral to receive loans. This feature allows people to receive credit who would not qualify with traditional financial institutions. As loans are repaid, usually in six months to a year, they are re-loaned. This continual reinvestment multiplies the impact of each dollar loaned.

For more information on microcredit loans, visit www.grameenfoundation.org.

Socially Responsible Investing

Some foundations match their investments to a particular cause or concern.

Socially responsible investing (SRI) allows foundations to invest their assets based on social and ethical considerations, integrating financial goals with personal values and societal concerns. For instance, a foundation that funds environmental issues might invest only in businesses that are environmentally conscious.

While many funds now screen for socially responsible funds, two of the oldest are Calvert (www.calvertgroup.com) and Domini (www.domini.com).

For a sample social responsible investment policy, see the end of this chapter.

Proxy/Voting/Shareholder Resolutions

Foundations generally commit 5 percent of their endowment annually to support their mission. But how many consider the potential embedded in the remaining 95 percent to promote the same mission?

Some people say active proxy voting is a way to put more power behind your invested dollars. Active proxy voting simply means that you:

1. Pay attention to issues raised by shareholders that have corporate governance or social implications for foundations.

2. Develop a position on them.

3. Ensure that your foundation casts a vote so its voice is heard.

A recent Council on Foundations survey suggests that most foundations have *not* instituted specific proxy voting policies for publicly traded companies held in their investment portfolios. A proxy voting policy can boost philanthropic mission in two important ways:

- It supports actions that seek to strengthen management at publicly traded companies, protecting long-term shareholder value and the value of foundation endowments.

- It has the potential to strengthen a foundation's charitable mission by using proxy voting to support social and environmental goals that are often at the heart of a foundation's work.

According to a report on proxy voting by the Rockefeller Philanthropy Advisors, many shareholders do not study their investments or consciously vote their proxies. Passive foundation shareholders also lose an important opportunity to send a clear message to corporations about social issues often directly relevant to their mission and areas of grantmaking.

Excerpts from the above taken from Unlocking the Power of the Proxy: How Active Foundation Proxy Voting Can Protect Endowments and Boost Philanthropic Missions. *Rockefeller Philanthropy Advisors, 2004. Visit* www.rockpa.org.

"Foundations are major investors in corporate America. We need to recognize and exercise the responsibilities of ownership. We can vote our values with our investment dollars, but the real leverage for change is an asset that most foundations ignore—the proxy vote."

—Lance Lindblom, president,
The Nathan Cummings
Foundation

J. Convene community leaders, nonprofits and/or other funders doing similar work.

Convening has been called a grantmaker's most underrated tool. It gives you the ability to draw together busy, knowledgeable people to discuss an important issue—and then perhaps encourage them toward a plan for action.

Convening is the act of bringing together a group of people for a clear, common purpose.

It creates the opportunity for dialogue and learning around an issue of mutual interest, for the benefit of all participants. Through a dialogue such as this, you can learn about the community or a particular issue, and where your foundation's support is needed most.

For example, if you ask your community's child care agencies to discuss the service needs for parents on welfare, this gathering would be called a convening.

Foundations are in the rare position of having a bird's eye view on the communities and fields they fund and are often in the best position to bring people together for mutual learning, coalition building and goal setting. As a convener, your foundation can introduce people who otherwise may not meet. By bringing different points of view together, you engage the broader community and provide an opportunity for change. Convening can also build relationships with your grantees. When you invite grantees to speak or attend a convening, you show them that you care about their opinion and want to learn from them.

Convening can take many forms, from informal meetings to elaborate events. Some examples include:

- Meetings
- Brown bag presentations
- Workshops
- Social events
- Luncheons
- Focus groups
- Listening sessions
- Open houses
- In-service trainings
- Facilitated panels or debates

Your foundation might convene nonprofits, grantmakers, community members, experts, researchers or more in any one of the above types of meetings. Sometimes the more simple affair, the better. A luncheon or half-day seminar, for example, can be surprisingly effective for sharing information, discussing best practices, building relationships, strengthening partnerships and more.

Many grantmakers convene regular meetings with other funders to discuss programs and possibilities for joint ventures. Others have formed local associations of grantmakers and/or regional associations of grantmakers. *See www.givingforum.org to find your regional association.*

For more information on convening, read "The Art of Convening: Working Together With Our Nonprofit Partners," Grantmaking Basics II, Council on Foundations, 2004. Visit www.cof.org.

In Their Own Words

Convening the Experts

"The Meadows Foundation frequently convenes members of the community for briefings on major issues facing our state and its people. Recent topics have included public education, mental health and the environment. Most recently, when 396,000 evacuees arrived in Texas as a result of Hurricanes Katrina and Rita, we invited mental health experts, Red Cross officials and others working with evacuees to brief our staff and our foundation colleagues on the short and long-terms needs of those affected by the tragedies. The more informed we are about issues, the better foundations can address them through our grantmaking."

—*Linda P. Evans, president and CEO, The Meadows Foundation*

K. Engage in public policy advocacy as permitted by law.

Public policy work is any legally appropriate activity that aims to change or inform government laws, administrative practices, regulations or orders. It can comprise a wide range of activities including legislative lobbying, advocacy, public interest research, community organizing and more.

Often, when people think of public policy, they think of advocacy and lobbying. These are two types of public policy work that are similar, but not the same.

Advocacy is active support for an issue—the act of pleading or arguing for something.

It includes any activity that supports or opposes an overall cause or issue and is not restricted to working on legislative remedies for an issue. *Direct* lobbying, however, is more narrowly defined as any attempt to influence a specific legislative proposal or bill. As defined by the IRS, direct lobbying occurs when you call, write or meet with legislators or legislative staff, expressing a view on currently pending legislation. Grassroots lobbying occurs if you urge others to make those contacts.

Engaging in Advocacy and Lobbying

Foundations often avoid advocacy because it is confused with lobbying, and lobbying is more highly regulated. In reality, with the guidance of knowledgeable counsel, family foundations can feel comfortable engaging in a wide variety of advocacy that does not meet the IRS definition of lobbying. Including in these permissible activities are activities that would be lobbying but for the IRS specifically identifying them as exceptions to lobbying.

One such exception to lobbying used by family foundations is the nonpartisan analysis, study or research exception. This exception allows foundations to gather and provide information to legislators and the community about areas of interest to the foundation To qualify for this exemption, the communication must contain a full and fair discussion of the facts sufficient to permit individuals to reach their own independent conclusion about the matter. Another exception permits foundations to share their expertise on particular issues with legislators if it is in response to a written request from a legislative body to provide information on pending legislation. A third exception allows foundation to engage in "self-defense" lobbying. Under the self-defense exception, foundations may directly communicate with legislators and legislative staff about issues that impact the foundation's existence, powers, duties or tax-exempt status.

See chapter 7 for more information on self-defense lobbying.

As long as the activity does ***not*** qualify as direct lobbying or grassroots lobbying or partisan political activity, your foundation can:

- **Convene** grantees, policymakers or other interested persons to discuss a particular legislative or other policy issue.
- **Educate the public on issues**, by writing letters to the editor, putting information up on your website, hosting a public forum or taking out ads.
- **Meet your legislators** to introduce them to your foundation and its work in the community.
- **Train grantees** on how to be effective advocates and lobbyists.
- **Comment on proposed regulations** or other administrative matters.

- **Bring lawsuits or participate in a friend of the court brief** (*amicus curiae*) in an effort to change laws or policies

- **Engage in nonpartisan voter education efforts.** Reminder: Under no circumstances can private foundations or public charities support or oppose candidates for public office or political parties.

Funding Advocacy

You can make grants to public charities that attempt to influence legislation, as long as your grants are not earmarked to support their lobbying efforts. ("Earmarking" is any written or oral agreement that funds will be used in a particular manner.) Private foundations may award general support grants to public charities even if the charities engage in lobbying activity. Private foundations may also award project grants to charities—even if the project includes some lobbying—so long as the amount of the grant does not exceed the grantee's budget for the non-lobbying components of the project.

Following these rules for permissible funding, The George Gund Foundation made a $50,000 grant to a state association of Ohio Food banks, who successfully lobbied legislators to include an $11 million line item in the state budget for increased emergency funding. And that's not all. The Gund Foundation made policy advocacy grants worth less than $150,000 to a state homeless coalition, which then persuaded lawmakers to create a $100 million housing trust for the state's homeless population. Supporting advocacy allowed this foundation's grantees to leverage the grant funds for a larger impact on their communities.

A growing number of family foundations understand that public policy advocacy is a great way to leverage their grant-making. Whether they make general support grants to groups that perform advocacy work, fund research on an issue or facilitate meetings around a certain agenda, many have found that advocacy work addresses problems more at their root.

For more information on how to engage in public policy advocacy, visit www.cof.org Public Policy or Legal, or contact the Council's Government Relations department at government@cof.org.

Peer Practices

Community Conversations Leads to Change

In 1995, the William Caspar Graustein Memorial Fund hired a demographer to conduct a study about the state of childhood education in Connecticut. The Graustein Fund's report on its findings generated 200 newspaper articles nationwide. But the organization didn't stop there. It held eight "community conversations" around the state, working with local boards of education, parent groups and teacher groups, and asked people to discuss the report. "It gave people a different way of approaching these issues and finding a common ground," said Nancy Leonard, public affairs officer with the fund.

Building on its initial success, the Graustein Fund held meetings in seven towns to discuss a proposed statewide school readiness act. State legislative staff attended the meetings and asked the communities to provide critical cost data on providing early childhood education. With help from Graustein staff, the citizens prepared the database in just two weeks, and Executive Director David Nee testified before the state legislature about the database and the meetings. "The school readiness bill passed and at least one legislator remarked, 'No Graustein Memorial Fund, no school readiness act.'"

In sum, ask yourself:

- Is my board doing everything it can to further our foundation's mission?

- Are we giving the right kind of financial support?

- What tools can we use to further our mission, beyond grants?

- What do key people really think about our foundation and our grantmaking process?

- What opportunities exist to align and ally with similar foundations and other nonprofits?

Resources

Family Matters newsletters:
- "Capacity Building Strategies" (Spring 2002)
- "Disaster Grantmaking" (Spring 2003)
- "Giving in Alternative Ways" (Spring 2001)
- "Small Grants" (Winter 2003)

Visit www.cof.org.

Funding and Engaging in Advocacy: Opportunities for Small Foundations. Association of Small Foundations, 2005. Visit www.smallfoundations.org.

Grantmaking Basics: A Field Guide for Funders. Council on Foundations, 1999. Item #509. Visit www.cof.org/publications.

Grantmaking Basics II: A Field Guide for Funders. Council on Foundations, 2004. Item #510. Visit www.cof.org/publications.

Grants to Individuals by Private Foundations. Council on Foundations, 1996. Item #803. Visit www.cof.org/publications.

The Guide to Successful Small Grants Program: When a Little Goes a Long Way. Council on Foundations, 2003. Item #870. Visit www.cof.org/publications.

A Funder's Guide to Advocacy. Fieldstone Alliance, forthcoming. Visit www.fieldstonealliance.org.

"What the Law Allows." *Foundation News & Commentary,* May/June 1997. Visit www.foundationnews.org.

"Election Year Politics." *Foundation News & Commentary,* July/August 2004. Visit www.foundationnews.org.

Websites

Alliance for Justice—National association of environmental, civil rights, mental health, women's, children's and consumer advocacy organizations. Visit www.allianceforjustice.org.

Center for Lobbying in the Public Interest—CLPI promotes, supports and protects nonprofit advocacy and lobbying to strengthen participation in democratic society and advance charitable missions. Visit www.clpi.org.

Charitable Reform Resource Center—Provides issue papers, talking points and sample letters for foundations to interact with their elected officials. Visit www.cof.org/Government Relations.

Public Policy Grantmaking Toolkit—Northern California Grantmakers offers this toolkit on public policy grantmaking to help funders engage in public policy initiatives. Visit www.ncg.org/toolkit/home.html.

Sample Grant Evaluation Form

Courtesy of the Leighty Foundation

Grant Evaluation Report

Success is measured in many different ways. Your evaluation is a critical tool for us. We hope it will be helpful for your organization as well. About 10 months after receiving your grant, we will plan to meet with you in person or by phone to discuss the grant. We ask that you complete the written evaluation and send it to us by (date).

Please begin your Evaluation Report with the following heading:

- Organization
- Project name (if applicable)
- Address
- Contact person
- Phone, fax, e-mail
- Date of grant award
- Grant amount
- Date of this report

1. Summarize the impacts and outcomes as they relate to this grant.
2. Were you able to accomplish the objectives you originally set? Evaluate each one.
3. Did you collaborate with any other organizations? Tell us about it.
4. What role did volunteers play in producing your outcomes?
5. What have you learned from your experience this year? What would you do differently?
6. What are your specific plans, if any, for continuing work on this program? How will you fund your efforts?
7. What one piece of advice would you give to The Leighty Foundation to help us serve our grantees more effectively?

Please submit your written evaluation by (date), by e-mail, attached file, to the XYZfoundation@xyz.org.

Sample Grantee Convening Letter
Courtesy of the Z. Smith Reynolds Foundation

(Date)

Dear _____:

In our travels across North Carolina, the staff of the Z. Smith Reynolds Foundation has the opportunity to learn about the many needs and challenges of the people of this state. We are often struck by the common goals and obstacles facing nonprofits and the incredible potential for cooperation.

Thus, we would like to invite you to a small gathering of nonprofit leaders to discuss your organization's agenda for 2005. In particular, we are interested in providing a forum for nonprofit leaders to share a) information about what their organizations hope to accomplish in the coming year and b) what they believe are the obstacles or barriers to achieving their goals. We hope this discussion will allow you and others to discern whether or not there might be opportunities to collaborate or cooperate across agendas and issues.

We believe this small, informal gathering of approximately 25 individuals will provide a comfortable environment in which alliances might be built, resulting in the strengthening of the nonprofit sector. Attached, please find the list of invitees, which may give you some idea of the kinds of cross-sector issues we will be discussing. Please come prepared to spend a couple of minutes describing your organization's 2005 goals and desired accomplishments.

(Time, date, RSVP information included here.)

Sample Socially Responsible Investment Policy

Excerpts courtesy the Lydia B. Stokes Foundation

Statement of Philosophy:

Corporations are more than institutions for making money. They do not operate in a vacuum. They can provide quality and service, and promote innovation in their products. They can make efforts to improve the lives of their workers and the communities in which they are located. They can change their practices to diminish pollution and other negative environmental impacts. Because the purpose of this Foundation is to promote improved quality of life for both people and the environment, we believe the portfolio should be invested in companies which make consistent, committed efforts to be socially responsible, as defined in our guidelines. We will seek out companies whose products, services, and methods of conducting business enhance the human condition and sustain our natural environment.

We recognize that no company is perfect, and that companies may excel in one social criteria and lag behind in another. We will look for quality of corporate disclosure, consistent efforts to be responsive to social concerns and changes, and environmental impacts as we evaluate investments on an individual basis for their ethical suitability.

Use of Social and Environmental Investment Criteria

The portfolio manager will judge potential portfolio additions or changes on their quality, financial soundness, effect on asset mix, and congruency with the Foundation's social and environmental criteria guidelines. Since companies are often involved in controversies around areas of qualitative concern, the portfolio manager is requested to discuss with the investment committee, any confusion or question about the intent of that criterion.

Social Justice Concerns

The account shall **avoid** domestic investments in companies with the following characteristics:

- derivation of more than 5 % of revenues from alcohol production and distribution
- any involvement in tobacco production or processing
- derivation of more than 3 % of revenues from the sale of tobacco products
- gambling services, and production and manufacture of gambling equipment
- genetic engineering and genetically modified products
- animal testing unless accredited by the AAALAC or the National Institutes of Health
- manufacture and distribution of weapons of war and/or weapons whose sole purpose is to kill people (not including hunting guns)
- derivation of more than 3 % of revenue from the Department of Defense. This criterion does not apply to goods and services that have no direct military purpose. The Foundation wishes to avoid companies providing weapons and other goods or services created solely for the purpose of harming people or the earth.

Environmental Concerns

The account shall **avoid** investments in companies with the following characteristics:

- disregard for a clean, healthy and sustainable environment; i.e. polluting, not disclosing information, substantially or repeatedly violating air water, hazardous waste management, or other environmental regulations
- nuclear power generation or processing
- refusing to change harmful production methods or practices when alternative technologies or practices are available.
- high toxic emissions levels in relation to their peer group
- production of ozone-depleting and agricultural chemicals
- derivation of revenues from the sale or combustion of coal or oil and their derivative fuel products
- extractive fossil fuel companies, except for natural gas

International Investing

The account shall **avoid** international investments with the following characteristics:

- strategic support for repressive regimes
- sweatshop labor, including unacceptable labor conditions and practices and use of forced labor or child labor
- conflict with indigenous peoples
- use of chemicals, pesticides, drugs, or environmental abuse which would be banned in the United States
- operational support of the government in Burma

Corporate practices abroad should be carefully examined. If any doubts exist, the Investment Manager should consult with the Investment Committee to decide whether to invest, divest, or file shareholder resolutions/protest.

Affirmative Screening

The account shall **seek out** socially responsible investments in companies that have the following characteristics:

- pro-active environmental policies
- a focus on alternative energy
- a focus on sustainable agriculture
- pro-active employment policies
- commitment to community affairs and charitable giving
- signing the CERES Principles
- a diverse board of directors with regard to gender and race
- reasonable compensation packages for CEOs relative to other employees

Continued on page 66

Community Investing

The Foundation considers community investing to be an additional way to align our assets with our mission, and to leverage our grantmaking activity. Therefore, we will designate a percentage of the average annual market value of the portfolio to community investing. This is currently set at 1%.

Shareholder Activities

Shareholder activities are a component of aligning the socially responsible investment guidelines with the investment activities. Voting on the proxies, co-filing, and filing shareholder resolutions are all part of this effort. Proxies shall be voted in accord with the concerns stated in the policy guidelines.

Proxies shall be voted in opposition of the following corporate board characteristics and actions:

- incentive payments unrelated to financial performance
- increasing salaries and options for executives that far exceed salary increases for average company employees
- boards composed mostly of "inside directors"
- nominating and compensation committees that are not composed exclusively of independent directors
- board nominees who serve on multiple (more than 3) boards, when the boards have many of the same people
- lack of diversity by gender, race and age
- golden parachutes for executives
- pension plans for non-employee directors

Investment Policy Review

All goals, objectives and policies will be in effect until modified by the investment committee.

The committee shall review the investment policy at least once every three years.

If, at any time, the investment manager believes that any policy guideline prevents him/her from meeting the performance objectives, or if he/she believes changing market conditions warrant consideration of revisions, it is the manager's responsibility to communicate those concerns clearly to the committee.

CHAPTER 4
Oversee Finances

PRINCIPLE IV:

OUR GOVERNING BOARD EXERCISES ACTIVE FISCAL OVERSIGHT.

Okay, take a deep breath. You've made it this far on the governance principles, and you're doing great.

Now you're about to enter into the World of Numbers. This is a world that speaks in a strange, stern language—with words like fiduciary and fiscal, compliance and control. Here you'll learn about what's diligent, what's reasonable, what's necessary—and what-you-had-better-be-doing-or-else, if you don't want to break the law.

If you're not a financial expert, this can be a scary world. But it's time to conquer your fear of finances—because if you're a member of the board, you're required to make sure the foundation's money is well spent.

When you join a foundation board, you are what's called a fiduciary—a steward of the foundation's assets. As a fiduciary, you have a responsibility to invest money and act wisely on behalf of the foundation. It's your job to make sure your foundation complies with federal, state and local laws.

You must educate yourself and your board on the legal and financial requirements for private foundations. This chapter will remind you of some of those requirements. However, the information here is not meant to replace legal advice or other, more comprehensive resources in these areas. Be sure to contact your attorney with any specific questions about how the laws pertaining to foundations apply to your foundation's activities.

If you are just forming a private foundation, consult First Steps in Starting a Foundation, *Fifth Edition, Council on Foundations, 2002. Visit www.cof.org.*

IN THIS CHAPTER

- Understand your fiduciary duties
- Prepare a budget and track expenses
- Perform due diligence on grants
- Establish effective internal controls
- Learn which records to keep
- Review and audit your finances
- Form an audit committee.

PRACTICE OPTIONS FOR PRINCIPLE IV

A. KNOW AND ENSURE COMPLIANCE WITH FIDUCIARY DUTIES.

Your board is legally responsible for investing money and acting wisely on behalf of the foundation. Recent corporate scandals have focused public attention on accountability, including at nonprofits. As a member of the board, you are responsible for demonstrating this accountability—and making sure your foundation meets its legal responsibilities.

As a fiduciary, you have two primary duties in managing the foundation's assets:

> **1) Duty of Care** means exercising your best judgment when making decisions. Perfection isn't required, but reasonable caution is. In short, the duty of care demands active participation and thoughtful attention to the foundation by individual board members. You can fulfill this duty by learning about the foundation's programs, attending meetings, participating in discussions and making sure you obtain the necessary information to ask questions.

> **2) Duty of Loyalty** means putting aside your personal and professional interests for the good of the organization. When you enter the boardroom, you are expected to focus exclusively on what's best for the foundation. A conflict-of-interest policy, signed annually by each board members is one way to ensure this duty of loyalty. *For more information on conflicts, see chapter 5.*

Fiduciary duty requires board members to stay objective, unselfish, responsible, honest, trustworthy and efficient. Board members must always act for the good of the organization, rather than for the benefit of themselves, and they need to exercise reasonable care in all decisionmaking.

Not every board member can be a financial wizard. However, every board member needs to know how the foundation manages its finances. It helps to understand basic terminology, to be able to read financial statements and to recognize errors and warning signs.

How do you know if your foundation is in good financial health? Ask yourselves:

- Does the budget support the overall strategy and goals of the foundation?
- Is the cash flow projected to be adequate?
- Do we have sufficient reserves?
- Are our permanent funds growing?
- Are we meeting, or exceeding, the minimum distribution requirement? (See below for more information.)
- Do we regularly compare financial activity with what has been budgeted?
- What areas of the budget have the most flexibility?
- Are our expenses reasonable and necessary? How do they relate to operations?
- Do we have the appropriate checks and balances to prevent errors, fraud and abuse?
- Do we have a process in place that ensures compliance with our mission?
- What policies and practices do you have in place for approval of expenses, increase/decrease in administrative fees and use of reserves?

What Is Payout?

The minimum distribution requirement, also called *payout*, refers to the federal requirement that private foundations distribute 5 percent of their assets each year for grants and administrative expenses.

The IRS requires that private foundations spend approximately 5 percent of their net investment assets as a payout requirement each year. Payout generally includes:

- Grants to public charities, nonprofits and individuals (including scholarships or emergency aid).
- Administrative expenses that help achieve your foundation's charitable purpose.
- Equipment that helps you achieve your foundation's charitable purpose.
- Direct charitable activities, such as meetings, research, publications and communications.

Each year, your foundation must meet the minimum payout requirement. Note that the following expenses *do not* count toward the 5 percent payout:

- Investment management fees.
- Custodial fees.
- Salaries or board meeting expenses to oversee investments.

It should be noted that your foundation may spend more than the minimum 5 percent to run its program. This decision will be based on your foundation's spending policy and its goals for perpetuity.

Also note that assets held for charitable purposes (a building that houses an art museum or research library operated by the foundation, for example) will not count as an investment asset on which the 5 percent minimum distribution amount will be figured.

B. ENSURE THAT EXPENSES ARE REASONABLE AND IN PROPORTION TO AMOUNTS SPENT ON GRANTS AND TECHNICAL ASSISTANCE.

As a fiduciary, overseeing the foundation's expenses is a critical part of your job. You and your board should ensure that expenses are reasonable and necessary. You should also ensure they are in proportion to the amount you spend on grants and technical assistance.

But how do you know what's "reasonable and necessary"?

According to the Tax Code, reasonable and necessary describes those expenses that are necessary for the foundation and not out of proportion to what similarly situated organizations are paying for similar services. If that definition doesn't clarify the issue for you, don't feel alone. It's sometimes difficult to determine what expenses are appropriate, and the assessment may depend on your foundation's activities and finances and the role that trustees and employees play.

Foundation expenses usually fall into three categories: operating expenses, grants expenses and investment management expenses. In section A, you read about your foundation's payout requirement, and what expenses can—and can not—be counted toward that requirement. Operating and grants expenses generally count toward the foundation's payout; investment management expenses, custodial fees, and expenses for meetings related to investments *do not* count toward a foundation's payout. *All* expenses should be reasonable and necessary.

Typically, the following operating and grants expenses of family foundations will count toward the foundation's payout:

- Grants to public charities, nonprofits and individuals (including scholarships or emergency aid).
- Office space and related expenses.
- Administrative expenses that help achieve your foundation's charitable purpose.
- Equipment that helps you achieve your foundation's charitable purpose.
- Direct charitable activities, such as convening, research, publications and communications.
- Compensation and benefits for staff (other than payments related to investment management).
- Compensation for board, if any (other than payments related to investment management).
- Legal and professional fees, including accounting, foundation management and/or consultants (other than payments related to investment management).
- Insurance.
- Interest, taxes and depreciation.
- Travel and out-of-pocket expenses for board members, staff and consultants (other than payments related to investment management).
- Printing.
- Memberships and dues.
- Meeting-related expenses.

Costs associated with investment management will offset investment income and therefore the amount of the foundation's excise tax on net investment income (generally 2 percent).

The costs for operating your foundation and making grants should be comparable to foundations of similar asset size, staff size and location. Refer to the Council's *Foundation Management Series, Foundation Governing Boards and Administrative Expenses in Private Foundations*. Visit www.cof.org.

Remember, though, that what seems reasonable and necessary to one group of people may seem stingy to some or lavish to others. Need a good test? Before you undertake an expense, ask yourself whether you would feel comfortable justifying that expenditure to your board, the IRS, a state attorney general or a reporter from the local newspaper.

C. EXPECT BOARD MEMBERS TO SERVE THE FOUNDATION WITHOUT COMPENSATION, RECOGNIZING THAT 1) REIMBURSEMENT OF REASONABLE EXPENSES DIRECTLY RELATED TO BOARD SERVICE DOES NOT CONSTITUTE COMPENSATION, AND 2) THAT BOARD MEMBERS WHO PERFORM STAFF FUNCTIONS MAY BE COMPENSATED AS STAFF.

Board compensation has been a touchy subject in the foundation field for some time. Some foundations consider it inappropriate to pay those serving on any nonprofit board. Others feel they need to provide compensation to attract and retain strong board members. Although many have made sound arguments both for and against compensation, best practice recommends *against* compensating trustees for routine board service.

Those against board compensation say it diminishes the good a foundation can do, as it takes financial resources away from grants. They say that foundations should hold the same standard they expect of grantees (who generally have volunteer boards) and that it is virtually impossible for a board to discuss the issue without it being a conflict of interest.

According to a recent Council on Foundations survey, 72 percent of family foundations *do not* compensate board members for their services. This reflects a common sentiment among family trustees that foundation work should be primarily a volunteer activity.

When a board reimburses its members for reasonable expenses directly related to board service, it is *not* considered compensation. (*See Expense Reimbursement Policy, below.*) Moreover, if a board member performs staff functions for the foundation, he or she may be compensated as staff. (*See Compensating Board Members Who Perform as Staff, below*).

Compensation Policy

Whatever your board decides about compensation and expense reimbursement, the current officers should create a policy to clarify the board's intention. With a clear policy in place, your board can avoid potential misunderstandings among trustees and have an objective way to respond to any compensation or reimbursement requests. The board should share this policy with prospective trustees in advance of their board service.

Your compensation policy can be a relatively simple statement describing 1) whether the board will or will not compensate trustees and, if it will, 2) what services it will compensate for (such as staff or administrative services and 3) how it will seek sufficient data to determine a reasonable compensation level.

If your foundation does compensate board members, it must set a reasonable compensation level—defined as the amount similar persons are paid for similar work at similar organizations. To determine what is reasonable, check other foundations in your region, of a similar size and assets, to compare what they do, or do not, pay their trustees. You should also check the Council on Foundation's *Grantmaker Salary and Benefits Survey*, available at www.cof.org.

Keep in mind that board compensation is public information, and your board must disclose what, if anything, it pays to trustees on its Form 990-PF tax return.

Compensating Board Members Who Perform as Staff

When setting the salary for a board member who serves as staff, your foundation should take special care to ensure that the level of compensation is reasonable. Most foundations rely heavily on salary surveys to guide them, such as the Council's *Grantmaker Salary and Benefits Survey*. Or, again, they compare compensation levels with foundations of similar size, operations and geographic location. To avoid a conflict of interest, any board members who serve as staff should be recused from the room when the board discusses, or votes on, their salaries.

> **What Is Reasonable?**
>
> The amount that similar persons are paid, at similar organizations, in a similar region.

In this era of intense scrutiny by Congress and the media, the Council urges all foundations to take great care in reviewing and approving the total compensation paid to its staff—particularly the top executive. When examples of excessive compensation come to light, they receive considerable media attention and negatively influence the perception of foundations and other charitable organizations in the minds of the public.

Expense Reimbursement Policy

Private foundations can pay for or reimburse ordinary and necessary expenses incurred in carrying out board activities—including the costs of travel by trustees.

Many foundations reimburse travel and out-of-pocket expenses, especially for those board members who may not have the individual resources to travel to foundation events. For example, they might reimburse trustees' expenses (airfare, hotel and meals) to attend a foundation board meeting. According to a recent Council on Foundations survey, more than half (59 percent) of family foundations reimburse board members for expenses to attend board meetings, and the same amount (59 percent) reimburse out-of-pocket expenses while members are on organization business.

When you reimburse trustees for travel and out-of-pocket expenses, you must be able to show the payment is: 1) reasonable and 2) for a necessary expense. Your board should state its reimbursement policy clearly and in writing, and include the following:

- Require that travel on behalf of the foundation be undertaken in a cost-effective manner. The law requires that these expenses not be "lavish or extravagant."

- State that the policy should be adhered to by anyone traveling or incurring expenses on behalf of the organization (for example, trustees, officers, employees, consultants, volunteers, etc.).

- State that expenses are reimbursable only if they are directly related to the foundation's work—and not personal activities.

- List what is—and what is not—reimbursable. For example, a foundation might pay for transportation, lodging and meals, but not pay for first-class travel.

- Describe the documentation required to receive reimbursement (e.g., itemized receipts) and who on the board will approve requests for reimbursement.

- State that the foundation will not pay for—nor reimburse travel or out-of-pocket expenses for—spouses, dependents or others, unless they, too, are performing official duties for the foundation.

- Special rules apply to many types of travel-related expenses and reimbursement. In this era of intense scrutiny on foundation expenditures, many foundations simply use the IRS guidelines to determine reasonable reimbursement rates (visit www.irs.gov/pub/irs_pdf/p1542.pdf for these guidelines).

Excerpts of the above taken from the Panel on the Nonprofit Sector: Final Report to Congress and the Nonprofit Sector, *June 2005.* Visit www.nonprofitsector.org.

For more information, see Developing a Travel Policy for Your Family Foundation, *By Jane C. Nober, Council on Foundations,* www.cof.org.

D. CONFIRM THAT PROPER DUE DILIGENCE IS PERFORMED TO ENSURE GRANTEES' FISCAL AND ORGANIZATIONAL VIABILITY AND THAT GRANTS ARE USED FOR CHARITABLE PURPOSES.

In grantmaking, due diligence describes the practice of reviewing grant requests before approving them. Due diligence means that, before making a grant, your foundation investigates prospective grantees to determine that they qualify to receive the grant.

Such an investigation enhances the likelihood that the project, if funded, will succeed.

Your foundation should develop and maintain a good due diligence process. The complexity of your foundation's process may vary, based on the size and scope of the grant, the number of your board or staff and your funding style. The key is to ask grantseekers for minimum information you need to determine: 1) that they are credible and fiscally sound organizations, and 2) that they will use your grant for charitable purposes.

For example, as a part of due diligence, a foundation might ask the following of its grant applicants:

- Can the organization provide an IRS letter of determination?
- Do they comply with applicable laws and regulations?
- Do they have the capacity to fulfill grant requirements?
- Do they manage their finances in a prudent manner?
- Is the budget within the means of the organization?
- Does the organization have the staff, experience and financial wherewithal to manage the project?
- Are they willing to provide you with the reports you require?

At the very minimum, you will want to verify that the organization is recognized by the IRS as a public charity. You can check GuideStar (www.guidestar.org), the National Database of Nonprofit Organizations, for information on the grant applicant and to view a copy of its Form 990 from previous years.

To assess an organization's fiscal health, foundations typically require a copy of the project budget along with an annual budget, balance sheet and income statement. Some foundations also request to see a copy of the organization's "independent auditor's report," also known as the auditor's opinion. If you do request an audit report, make sure it is signed and dated and look for any problem areas.

Speaking of problem areas—be sure to include in your due diligence process what to do if you doubt a grant applicant's eligibility. *How will you communicate that to the grantseeker? How much feedback or technical assistance will the foundation give?*

Due diligence doesn't stop with the application review process. Throughout the course of the grant period, you might ask grantees to provide you with midway progress reports and a final narrative and financial report. These reports help you monitor the use of the funds and also assess the effectiveness of the grant.

Due diligence, however, should not put an undue burden on the grantee. Your foundation should set requirements that respect grantee time and are reasonable in relation to the grant size. *For more information, see chapter 6.*

In Their Own Words

Offering Technical Assistance

"When we are performing due diligence, we offer grantees technical assistance if we see they need it. The staff and I will train people on payroll, how to pay bills, use a general ledger—we'll show them how to manage their books in a hands-on way. We do this because we've learned the hard way. We've funded grants before where money ends up missing. This allows us to know that the people we fund have controls in place."

—Susan Halliday, director of finance, Jacobs Family Foundation

Peer Practices

Involving the Community in Due Diligence

For one small foundation with limited staff, it was important to use volunteer resources to ensure due diligence. With staff guidance and oversight, the foundation solicited volunteer committee members to individually rank grants and research grant applicants. These rankings are then discussed at a committee meeting, and final grant recommendations are then brought before the board. This is an effective way for a small foundation to get the work done effectively, while involving community members. According to one foundation staff member, this practice has made their grantmaking well rounded because the review committee members come from different perspectives—both geographically and by area of interest.

E. Ensure that the foundation has a written investment policy adequate for its size and complexity that includes investment objectives, asset allocation strategy, spending and/or payout policy, and rationale for selecting and evaluating investment managers/advisors.

As part of your board fiduciary responsibilities, it's your job to seek out the best return and risk tolerance on investments. Fiduciary responsibility does not mean you must actively manage the foundation's assets, but you must actively monitor the process of managing them.

Most foundations delegate asset management to an external professional or firm, which then monitors investment performance and adheres to the directives of the foundation. Your foundation will provide these directives through written policies and procedures developed by the board, investment committee, staff or external professionals—in most cases, investment consultants.

Your board needs to define its spending and investment goals and understand its fiduciary responsibilities. As part of your board's investment responsibility, it should:

- Develop written investment strategy, including a policy and objectives
- Develop a spending and/or payout policy
- Set an asset allocation strategy
- Document the investment decisionmaking process
- Establish a return required to support the spending policy
- Employ skilled investment consultants and/or managers
- Articulate the rationale for selecting and evaluating these investment consultants and/or managers.

Spending Policy

A **spending policy** is the annual percentage of assets a foundation decides to spend on administration and grants. The policy describes restrictions on spending, how spending is calculated, and the controls in place to ensure compliance with the governing instruments and the donors' intent. Many foundations develop grants and administrative budgets based on their spending policy.

Your foundation must address a number of important questions when setting—or evaluating—the spending policy:

- Will the foundation exist in perpetuity?
- Is the foundation fully funded or will additional assets be received?
- Does the foundation board want to exceed the minimum payout requirement? If so, by how much?
- Does the board want to build the foundation's endowment? Or is it satisfied maintaining the value of the endowment on an inflation-adjusted ("real") basis?

- How can the foundation best achieve its program objectives: By spending more now? By constant and sustained effort over time? Or by growing the endowment so that more can be spent in the future?

- Does the policy reflect the philosophy of the donors and/or board of trustees?

Remember that at a minimum, your foundation *must* meet the 5 percent payout requirement. Most foundations calculate their spending by *starting with the minimum payout requirement* of 5 percent, and then considering other factors—such as the current year's income, past grant commitments and current grantee needs, additional administrative expenses, investment returns and more.

A good spending policy:

- Provides sufficient funds for operations and grants.

- Leaves sufficient funds for the assets to grow, at minimum, with inflation so that inflation-adjusted spending is perpetuated.

- Minimizes the impact of market volatility on year-to-year spending.

- Is clearly articulated and documented.

- Implies a challenging, but achievable, investment objective.

Investment Strategy

Once your foundation has developed a sound spending policy and objective, you can determine your investment strategy.

Family foundations manage investments differently depending on their size and structure. A wide variety of approaches and investment products may be used, including mutual funds, balanced portfolios, investments managers for specific asset classes, the use of passive indexed funds and investment collaboratives.

As part of your **investment strategy**, you and your board will need to:

1. **Calculate the rate of return you require.** This determines how much your foundation needs to achieve to maintain your endowment and meet your spending goals.

2. **Develop an overall asset allocation strategy.** Asset allocation is the practice of spreading risk (the possibility of losing or not gaining value) across a range of investment assets and management styles to balance the effect of a volatile market. Your asset allocation strategy will determine how well your portfolio performs.

3. **Develop the strategy and a written investment policy for the foundation.** Your foundation's investment strategy and policy helps guide the board, the investment committee (if there is one) and investment managers in managing the foundation's portfolio.

An **investment policy** is a written statement of the overall investment philosophy, describing what the foundation is trying to accomplish with its permanent funds. The policy lists individual investment objectives and describes how these contribute to the overall goals of the foundation. It includes the foundation's asset allocation criteria and its spending policy. The policy should also describe what is expected day-today of managers, as well as the standards to evaluate a manager's performance.

Your financial professional or legal counsel should help develop the investment policy. Although every foundation's policy will be different, each should contain the same basic points. Investment policies should:

- Define general objectives (such as preserve and protect the assets; achieve aggressive growth, etc.).

- Delegate day-to-day asset management.

- Describe asset allocation parameters and guidelines for diversification.

- Describe asset quality (itemize quality ratings for stocks, bonds, or short-term reserves based on your risk tolerance).

- Define who reviews investment performance and managers, the frequency and regularity of reviews, and how the foundation will document such reviews.

- Establish measures to evaluate investment performance.

- Include a spending policy.

For sample investment strategies and policy statements, see the samples at the end of this chapter, and visit the Stewardship Principles for Family Foundations at http://bestpractices.cof.org/family.

Excerpts of the above taken from Policy Making Made Clear: Eleven Policies Your Foundation Should Consider, *by Elaine Gast for the Association of Small Foundations, 2005. Visit www.smallfoundations.org.*

Peer Practices

Staying the Course When It Comes to Investments

The William J. and Dorothy K. O'Neill Foundation keeps to a basic investment philosophy: to be invested in stocks and fully invested at all times. According to President William J. O'Neill, Jr., "We're an all equity investor, but we diversify in many equities—large cap, mid cap, small cap, micro cap, emerging foreign markets and various types of alternative investments."

Because the foundation is intended to exist in perpetuity, it invests in stocks to get the greatest growth over a long time. "We don't feel we can time the market successfully—when to get in, when to get out, so we stay fully invested."

The foundation does, however, set aside two years of projected cash outflows into short-term, high-grade bond investments. O'Neill calls this the foundation's safety—a reserve fund. "As we draw money out of the foundation to pay grants, we take it out of our equity portfolio if the stock market is strong. If our stocks are tanked, however, we can use the money from the bonds."

"We believe this will let our portfolio grow over the years in real terms, after our grants and expenses."

F. Establish effective internal controls, systems of checks and balances, and formalized recordkeeping.

Your foundation needs certain internal systems to protect its funds and its important records. If your board hasn't established proper internal controls and a formalized records management system, now is the time. Doing this shows good management and will help you be prepared for an IRS audit or other investigation.

Internal Controls

Internal control mechanisms are not intended to detect fraud, but rather to prevent it. Establishing control mechanisms will help you:

- Oversee the foundation's governance and operations
- Manage knowledge regarding internal policies and procedures
- Protect tax status and preserve trustees' limited personal liability.

Typical control mechanisms include: 1) making sure there is clarity in job descriptions and responsibilities; 2) defining financial and accounting procedures [signing checks, handling of cash, approving expenses, outlining parameters for credit card usage], 3) establishing a system of checks and balances for all handling of cash and expenses, 4) managing potential conflicts of interest with a clear policy and 5) requesting regular independent audits.

Recordkeeping

In the past, foundations may not have paid much attention to the issue of recordkeeping. But with the passage of the Sarbanes-Oxley Act of 2002, the subject is one you shouldn't ignore. A good records management system will help you:

- Identify and safeguard important documents
- Organize, maintain and retrieve records
- Create an institutional memory relating to board decisions
- Prepare for an audit
- Preserve the foundation's history
- Train new trustees on the foundation's, background, policies and procedures.

In response to the recent legislation, every foundation should adopt a written policy on records retention. Your records retention policy should include the following:

- A list of documents the foundation will keep permanently, and those it will keep for a specified period of time.
- Guidelines for retaining and routinely purging information (including electronic records).
- A description of who will be in charge of retaining the records, and where they will be stored.

A records retention policy will help the foundation maintain accountability in the event of an audit or public questioning. Some small foundations delegate their recordkeeping duties to accountants, custodians or consultants. If your foundation does outsource these responsibilities, be sure trustees understand that it is *the board*—not the hired contractor—that is ultimately responsible for overseeing its operations and records.

The following are general guidelines as to the records your foundation should keep and for how long—not all of which are legal requirements. Although the IRS has published a *Compliance Guide for 501(c)(3) Tax-Exempt Organizations*, which broadly addresses recordkeeping for non-profits, there are no IRS rules on recordkeeping specific to foundations. Although there is no specific advice from the law, the Council on Foundations recommends the following best practices.

Keep these documents **permanently**:

- Original organization documents (articles of incorporation, trust instrument, bylaws, etc., plus any amendments to these documents).

- Form 1023, the application for federal tax-exempt status.

- Form SS-4, the application for taxpayer identification number.

- IRS favorable determination letter, which is the IRS ruling that 501(c)(3) status is granted.

- All Forms 990-PF, the foundation's annual tax return.

- Any official correspondence with the IRS.

- Foundation's annual reports.

- Any other tax exemption certificates—for example, from state or local authorities.

- Correspondence with attorneys, accountants and/or custodians of the foundation's assets.

- Board records, such as meeting minutes and committee actions.

In addition to the permanent records listed above, your foundation should keep some files on hand for **a certain period of time**:

- Grant files—keep for a minimum of six years in case of an audit.

- Record of contributions—keep until tax reporting is complete and the audit period has ended.

- Personnel records, as applicable—check with your attorney or accountant to determine the required length of time to retain these records.

- Financial records—keep investment reports until assets are sold and for the duration of the audit period; keep foundation transaction records for the tax reporting and audit period that follows.

- Contracts—in general, keep for three years after the contract expires.

Your records retention policy should call for a backup system in case of disaster. For paper files, this may mean storing additional copies of your permanent records off site or electronically. For electronic documents, make sure you regularly create computer backups.

Recordkeeping Tips from Your Colleagues

- Create a master list of grants and grant reports.

- Scan important documents to store them electronically.

- Start a reference file of local agencies and the services they provide.

- Consider starting an archive of your historical documents.

- Keep hard copies of legal documents (articles of incorporation, tax returns, bylaws) in a fire-safe place at a separate location.

- Back up your computer regularly.

- Set a regular schedule for purging inactive documents.

G. APPROVE AN ANNUAL BUDGET AND ASSESS THE FOUNDATION'S FINANCIAL PERFORMANCE RELATIVE TO THE APPROVED BUDGET.

Annual budgets are both a financial tool to help manage operations and a fiscal control mechanism. It is the board's responsibility to approve and monitor the annual budget and assess the financial performance relative to that budget. The budget will help you allocate resources wisely, meet payout obligations and avoid unexpected shortfalls or surpluses.

An administrative budget, as distinct from a grants budget, is your foundation's blueprint for yearly program objectives. There are a variety of ways to develop the administrative budget, including zero-based budgeting, base plus budgeting, departmental or cost center budgeting and more. Your foundation, in conjunction with your accountant, can determine which of these makes sense for the organization.

Most foundations find it helpful to divide the administrative budget according to various areas. Examples of line items might include:

Revenue:

- Investment returns
- Unrestricted contributions
- Interest on income
- Brokerage commission recapture
- Other.

Expenses:

- Salaries and benefits
- Professional development
- Fees for professional services
- Occupancy
- Office expenses
- Programmatic expenses
- Communications
- Travel and conferences
- Funds available for grantmaking
- Other expenses.

Peer Practices

Budgeting Software

The Hamilton-White Foundation wanted to get a better handle on where its non-grantmaking money was going. The board decided to create an annual budget that incorporated grants and operating expenses, said Phil White, former president of the foundation. "Previously, we only had an annual grantmaking budget. We moved to a budgeting software that let us plug in expenses, assets, liabilities and grants, as well as create reports. It was so simple, even a non-accounting person could use it."

The foundation's over-the-counter software called Peachtree stored the information and tracked expenses versus budget. "It also helped with our accountants and auditors, in case we were ever audited," said White. "Our accountants were able to prepare our tax returns based on me e-mailing them our financial statements. It reduced our accounting costs, because they spent less time preparing our taxes."

As a result of the change, White said the board gained a better understanding of the foundation's financial picture. "You don't need a really sophisticated system to create your annual budget," he said. "But you do need a system."

In addition to the administrative budget, some foundations develop a separate capital budget each year for equipment, facilities, etc.

The staff, accountant and/or board treasurer must report to the board on a regular basis about the foundation's financial health. They typically prepare monthly or quarterly financial statements, showing the annual budget, spending for the month just passed, total spending year to date and, perhaps, spending as a percentage of the total budget.

These regular reports inform the board on cash balances, significant amounts due to the foundation, and any acquisition or disposal of property. As your staff or board routinely monitors the administrative budget, it may be necessary to reallocate resources within that budget throughout the year.

You can best manage financial reporting through the use of software designed specifically for accounting and reporting. The best solution involves an integrated approach that addresses all aspects of the operations of a private foundation. There are many vendors offering foundation management software. *For suggestions, contact the Council on Foundations at family@cof.org.*

H. Conduct an internal review of foundation compliance with legal, regulatory and financial reporting requirements, and provide a summary of the review to board members.

Accountability means adhering to laws and regulations to ensure your foundation furthers its charitable mission. To demonstrate its accountability, your board should establish and carry out policies and procedures that demonstrate its transparency, credibility and integrity to the board, grantees and the community.

It is the board's responsibility to periodically review the foundation's policies and procedures to ensure compliance with legal and financial rules. Be sure to seek the help of an attorney who can keep you abreast of any changes in the law.

Some boards use a finance committee to monitor the details of foundation spending. The finance committee oversees the budget and annual operating plan and makes recommendations to the full board. It monitors the foundation's accounting policies and recommends financial guidelines. The finance committee also reports any financial irregularities, concerns or opportunities to the full board. It oversees compliance with bylaws and board policies and, generally speaking, protects the foundation, board and staff from undue risk.

As part of this regular review process, the finance committee should evaluate how well members of the board:

- Know the federal regulations and state laws.
- Understand their roles and responsibilities.
- Understand the Stewardship Principles for Family Foundations.
- Craft, communicate and enforce strong policies, including a conflict of interest policy and a code of ethics.
- Make 990-PFs easily available.
- Invest and monitor the foundation's money wisely.
- Set a policy on records management and make sure files are maintained appropriately.

- Document corporate meeting minutes.

- Publish an annual report with financial data.

- Apply due diligence in grantmaking.

- Conduct a self-evaluation on the overall effectiveness of the board and foundation.

If your board follows good governance practices such as those listed here, you will create an accountable and credible foundation—and one that avoids organizational crises.

In Their Own Words

Finance Committee Oversight

"Our finance committee meets quarterly to oversee the foundation's finances. As a part of their role, they approve the annual budget, review the quarterly financials and study and approve any significant financial commitment the foundation makes. In addition, they get reports on our portfolio twice a year. Our portfolio managers phone into the finance committee meetings twice per year to walk through the reports. As the director of finance, I prepare monthly updates on finance related issues, giving the board the opportunity to come back with questions."

—*Susan Halliday, director of finance, Jacobs Family Foundation*

Reviewing Policies to Ensure Compliance

"The Huston Foundation recently reviewed its policies and employee procedures. We used our law firm to make sure we were meeting all the legal requirements on our policies. After we revised some of our policies to meet the changes in the law, we made copies of our employee policies and board practices and distributed them in a handbook to the board and staff."

—*Charles Huston III, vice president of community relations & director of operations, The Huston Foundation*

I.

OBTAIN AN EXTERNAL REVIEW OF THE ORGANIZATION'S FINANCES (IN ACCORDANCE WITH ASSET SIZE) BY CONDUCTING A FINANCIAL REVIEW, PERIODIC AUDIT OR ANNUAL AUDIT (FOR LARGER FOUNDATIONS).

Although independent audits and financial reviews are not required, they provide important protection from possible liabilities. They ensure the accuracy of your foundation's financial statements and show donors the foundation is operating in an honest and efficient way. Audits confirm that your foundation exercises proper stewardship and that funds placed in its care are being used as the mission intends.

Your foundation should consider hiring an outside firm to conduct an independent audit or financial review—ideally, once a year, but at least once every three years. A financial review is less extensive than an audit, as it is a review of individual financial statements only. An audit examines the financial statements taken as a whole, in relation to the organization's internal control structure, investment policies, grantmaking and more.

The audit or financial review should be conducted by an independent public accountant with knowledge of nonprofit issues. Auditors should provide a written report highlighting any weaknesses or areas for improvement. Once your foundation receives its audit or financial review, you should make the results publicly available, for example, in your annual report or on your website.

There are different levels of audits and reviews. When hiring an external auditor, make sure it is clear at the start what the foundation will be paying for. Although some accountants give cost estimates for each aspect of the audit, others will simply give you one estimate for the audit and then add on costs at the end for preparation. Here are a few tips to help keep costs down:

Keep your records as automated as possible. This makes it easier for the auditor to access the information.

Keep ledgers as clean and clear as possible. If it is difficult for the accountant to decipher ledgers, it just means more time for them and more money out of the foundation's pocket.

Peer Practices

Voluntary Audits

The Samuel N. and Mary Castle Foundation wanted to show the public that it held itself to the same standards as its grantees, so it obtains an annual voluntary audit. "By opening up all of our books, procedures, selection processes, history and administrative costs, we are becoming a more user-friendly organization," said Al Castle, executive director and trustee. "Our transparency helps to send a clear message that it is we who work for our grantees and that we will never ask more of them in the way of accountability, efficiency or efficacy than we demand of ourselves."

The foundation placed its voluntary annual audit, including a statement by its independent auditor, on its website. "We want the public to evaluate our internal efficiency," explains Castle. "We direct all press inquiries to our audited fiscal statement on the Web."

Do your paperwork. Have staff or the board audit committee do the simple paperwork to avoid accumulating more costs during an audit.

One more tip: Consider rotating your auditor every five to seven years if possible, even though rotation may increase costs. This will demonstrate an even greater level of accountability in your auditing process.

J.

ESTABLISH AN AUDIT COMMITTEE TO OVERSEE ACCOUNTING, FINANCIAL REPORTING, COMPENSATION PRACTICES AND THE EXTERNAL AUDIT OF THE FOUNDATION.

Many larger grantmakers already follow the practice of public companies by using an audit committee to oversee the work of outside auditors. Foundations, particularly those that hold substantial assets or have large boards, should consider creating an audit committee to validate the organization's accounting practices and financial reporting. (In California, state law requires foundations to have an audit committee.)

When forming an audit committee, your board should adopt a charter setting forth the committee's powers and legal duties, as well as the required qualifications of the audit committee members.

An audit committee should include at least one "financial expert" from the board or outside the foundation. A financial expert, in this case, is someone who understands and can apply accounting principles, who understands internal controls and financial reporting and who understands the functions of an audit.

If your board doesn't have any members with sufficient financial expertise, and if state law permits, you may form a committee composed of all outside advisors. Even if your board does have someone with financial expertise, it's a good idea to include at least some members on the committee who are independent of the foundation.

What do audit committees do? An audit committee recommends and works with an outside auditor, ensuring they have full access to financial and related records. The committee reviews the audit report and arranges for the auditor to meet with the full board once a year. Once the audit is complete, the committee presents it to the full board.

Your foundation should weigh carefully whether the audit committee should also supervise the foundation's investment activities or whether those functions should be clearly separate.

See sample audit committee responsibilities at the end of this chapter.

In Their Own Words

What the Audit Committee Does

"According to the law in California, we have to issue an audited financial statement, have an independent auditor, make the results of our audit available to the public and have a separate audit committee. The chair of our finance committee serves on the audit committee (although not as chair), and we have two independent (non-board) members on the committee as well.

"The audit committee reports to the finance committee, which has the power to approve the audit committee's recommendations. For example, at the audit committee's first meeting, members discussed hiring an independent auditor and approved the engagement letter. The audit committee also works with the independent auditor to review the audit report.

"Next year, the audit committee will take the lead in commissioning an internal control study—something we do every other year."

—*Susan Halliday, director of finance, Jacobs Family Foundation*

In sum, ask yourself:

How aware are our board members and staff of their legal and fiduciary responsibilities?

Does my foundation comply with all Internal Revenue Service regulations?

How does my foundation make sure that our expenses are reasonable?

What due diligence do we perform on our grants?

What financial policies and practices are in place in our foundation? Do we have an approved annual budget, a written investment policy, sound recordkeeping and internal controls?

Do we periodically conduct an external review of our finances?

Resources

Conducting an Audit: Self-Assessment—An Online Tutorial. By Andrew Schulz, Thomas Raffa and Michael Hoehn. Council on Foundations, 2005. Visit www.cof.org.

Expenditure Responsibility: Step by Step, Third Edition. By John A. Edie. Council on Foundations, 2002. Item #824. Visit www.cof.org/publications.

Family Foundations and the Law, Third Edition. By John A. Edie. Council on Foundations, 2002. Item #806. Visit www.cof.org/publications.

"Fashioning an Investment Strategy." By Jason Born. *Splendid Legacy.* National Center for Family Philanthropy, 2002. Visit www.ncfp.org.

Financial Management for Nonprofits: Keys to Success. By Peter Konrad and Alys Novak. Regis School of Professional Studies, 2001. To order, call 800/798-4153.

Foundation Management Series, Foundation Governing Boards and Administrative Expenses in Private Foundations. Volume 11. Council on Foundations, 2004. Visit www.cof.org/publications.

Grantmaker Salary and Benefits Report. Council on Foundations. Visit www.cof.org/publications.

"Hands On: Keep, File, Toss?" By Jane C. Nober. *Foundation News & Commentary,* March/April 1998: 47–49. Visit www.foundationnews.org.

"Investing Wisely." *Family Matters* (Winter 2002). Visit www.cof.org.

Spending Policies and Investment Planning for Foundations: A Structure for Determining a Foundation's Asset Mix. By DeMarche Associates. Council on Foundations, 1999. Visit www.cof.org/publications.

"Thinking About an Audit?" By Andras Kosaras. *Foundation News & Commentary,* July/August 2005. Visit www.foundationnews.org.

Top Ten Ways Family Foundations Get Into Trouble, Second Edition. By Ellen Bryson and John A. Edie. Council on Foundations, 2004. Item #849. Visit www.cof.org/publications.

Sample Foundation Policy Acknowledgment

Courtesy of the Americana Foundation

I, _____, a trustee of the _____ Foundation acknowledge that I have received, understand and have agreed that the following are approved policies of the Americana Foundation and that they are to be adhered to through all actions of the board and staff. In addition, I will insure that all actions of the foundation will comply with applicable state and federal rules and regulations.

The following policies apply to the above statement:

Internal Controls Policy

Saved Documents Policy

The Travel and Reimbursement Policy

The Conflict of Interest Policy

Audit Committee Roles and Responsibilities

The Investment Policy

Signature:_____

Date:_____

Sample Administrative Cash Flow Sheet

Courtesy of the Atkinson Foundation

	Approved 2006 Budget	Actual YTD 8/31/06	Projected 2007	Expenditure Approved 2007
Budget				
SALARIES AND ALLOWANCES				
Professional Staff				
Support Staff				
Medical and Group Insurance				
Vision Care (self-insured)				
Retirement Annuity				
Tuition Reimbursement				
FICA Expense				
Unemployment/Disability				
Other Fees and Temps/Consultants				
SUBTOTAL				
OFFICE AND RELATED EXPEN.				
Payroll Expenses				
Professional Fees—Audit/Accountant				
Insurance—Office, Liability, Bonding				
General Expense				
Postage and Mailing				
Printing, Stationery, Supplies				
Rent				
Equipment Expenses—Lease/Maintenance				
Legal				
SUBTOTAL				
PROGRAM DEVELOPMENT				
Guidelines/Publication				
Conference and Training				
Board Meeting				
Other Trustee Meetings and Expense				
Trustee Training				
Library and Periodicals				
Hospitality				
Telephone and Telegraph				
Memberships				
Miscellaneous				
SUBTOTAL				
STAFF TRAVEL & MEETINGS				
DEPRECIATION EXPENSE				
CAPITAL EXPENSE				
TOTAL				

Sample Travel and Expense Guidelines

Courtesy of the Americana Foundation

The Foundation shall pay or reimburse the ordinary, necessary and reasonable cost of hotel accommodations. "Deluxe" or "luxury" hotel rates are not to be paid or reimbursed. Trustees and employees shall obtain a rate at least equivalent to the hotel's corporate or discount rate. The above rates are 2001 top corporate rate ranges for major metropolitan areas and should be used as a guide in determining reasonable cost. (These rates shall be surveyed on an annual basis and be reviewed by the trustees.)

On occasions when a particular hotel is the site of a convention or other event sponsored by another entity, the rates charged by the hotel may be a reimbursable expense, but the cost of such hotel will be a factor in the foundation's determination of whether to have trustees or employees attend such event. Expenses for travel, lodging and meals will be reimbursed by the foundation for trustees and staff approved to represent the foundation.

The foundation will not pay for the additional cost above normal room rates for hotel suites unless such accommodations are used for meetings for Foundation business. The use of a suite shall require the prior approval of the Executive Director.

SPOUSAL EXPENSES

If the spouse of a trustee accompanies him/her on a business trip for the foundation, the spouse's expenses cannot be charged to the foundation.

AIR TRANSPORTATION

Air fares shall be coach class and should take advantage of early booking rates (seven and fourteen day advance) and Saturday night stay when possible.

AUTO RENTALS AND MILEAGE

Rentals are at the mid-sized rate

Private car use   0.36.5 per mile

REIMBURSEMENT PAYMENTS

Reimbursements for meetings and related expenses shall be submitted on the foundation standard form with receipts attached within 40 days of the meeting or event. Costs incurred during the fiscal year must be received by January 31 to facilitate the closing of the books.

Trustees who participate in grantee site visits at the request of the executive director will be reimbursed for expenses related to the visit. Expenses shall be listed and receipts attached to the reimbursement form.

LOCATION OF BOARD MEETINGS

Meetings of the board of trustees shall be held at Novi, Michigan. The primary factors to be considered in selecting alternative locations for board meetings, including committee meetings of the board, shall be (1) the programs and purposes of the meetings and (2) the cost thereof.

When committee meetings are held at times other than full Board meetings, the committee shall approve in advance the site and date of the meeting. The committee meeting minutes shall specify the purpose of the meeting and reason for the site selected, if other than at Tollgate Farm.

Sample Investment Policy

Courtesy the Mellam Family Foundation

Overview

The following statement of general investment objectives and guidelines are the policies, which govern the overall management of the Mellam Family Foundation's (the Foundation) assets managed by XXX.

The primary investment objective is the preservation of principal, including the effects of inflation, and secondarily providing for growth while minimizing interim volatility. In a down market the preference is to take a more "defensive" posture with respect to principal preservation (i.e., more fixed income exposure and less equity exposure), with the realization that we may miss some of the upside when the market recovers. This is the reason for the wide asset allocation targets (see below).

Asset allocation guidelines

The asset allocation guidelines are designed to achieve the Foundation's long-term appreciation objectives and are reviewed periodically in light of market changes and opportunities by the board of the Foundation. At a minimum the guidelines will be reviewed during the fourth quarter board meeting.

The current asset allocation guidelines are as follows:

Asset Category	Allocation
Equities	50-70%
Fixed Income	20-45%
Alternate Investments	0-5%
Cash Equivalents	0-10%

The overall structure of the portfolio shall be targeted to the ratios reflected above thereby giving the portfolio manager broad discretion within each asset category to adjust the portfolio in response to market conditions.

Liquidity requirement

Liquidity will be provided as necessary for charitable payouts and operating expenses.

Investment Policies

1. Equity investments will be made from a stable, long-term perspective with moderate annual turnover.

2. The purpose of equity investments are to provide appreciation of principal which more than offsets inflation and to provide for maximum total return, while also recognizing the need for capital preservation. It is recognized that equity investments generally entail the assumption of relatively greater market variability and risk than a portfolio entirely invested in debt securities.

Continued on page 90

3. All investment securities, both equity and fixed income, shall represent seasoned, high quality companies or entities.

4. In recognition of the benefits of commingled funds as investment vehicles (i.e., the ability to diversify more extensively), the investment manager may from time to time elect to invest in mutual funds managed directly by UST.

Equity guidelines:

- The investment manager will maintain a diversified portfolio of stocks at all times.
- A minimum of 40 different companies and most S&P sectors will be represented in the portfolio. Sector weightings are limited to the S&P weight +/- 5 percentage points.
- A single security many not compromise more than 5% (at market) of the equity portfolio for a sustained period.
- International equities (individual securities or mutual funds) shall not comprise more than 15% of the total equity holdings.
- No more than 5% of a corporation's outstanding issues in a given security class may be purchased.
- Short sales and merger purchases are prohibited.

Fixed income guidelines:

- Non-government (or government agency) issues must be investment grade (rated at least BAA by Moody's or BBB by S&P) at time of purchase, with a preference for an average credit rating of A or better.
- Fixed income maturities will be laddered to minimize reinvestment risk and the average duration of the portfolio of individual securities held should not be longer than 8 years.
- A single security (excluding Government issues) may not comprise more than 10% of the portfolio at cost.
- Cash and cash equivalents will be in money market funds or securities rated P-1 by Moody's or A-1 by S&P.

Performance benchmarks

Asset	Benchmark
Domestic equity	S&P 500 Index
International equity	Financial Times World X-US Index
Fixed income	Lehman Brothers Credit Bond Index
Cash	3-month Treasury Bills
Other (Hedge Fund)	HFR Fund of Funds Index

Investment results will be monitored on an ongoing basis but evaluated on a longer-term basis over a period of 2 to 3 years.

Reporting guidelines

The investment manager will provide portfolio performance reports to the Executive Director on a quarterly basis. These reports will outline asset category performance (and respective benchmarks) for the just competed quarter, year-to-date, prior year, prior 3 years, prior 5 years, and inception-to-date. Accompanying these quarterly portfolio reports will be narrative comments by the investment manager highlighting significant transactions, events, trends or other information the investment manager determines are noteworthy and of interest to the board. This information will be included in the quarterly expense and financial statement information prepared by the Executive Director.

The investment manager will attend the June and December board meetings to review investment performance and answer questions from the board. Prior to these meetings the investment manager will distribute portfolio performance reports (as described above) and other information he deems appropriate to the board members for the most currently available reporting period. At the board's discretion the investment manager may be asked to report at other quarterly meetings during the year.

Sample Audit Committee Roles and Responsibilities

Courtesy the Americana Foundation

The President of Americana Foundation shall appoint the members of the Audit Committee. The committee shall be composed of at least three trustees with one being the president of the board. The committee shall perform its duties totally independently of the Finance Committee. No member of the Audit Committee will accept compensation from the foundation for providing services other than as a member of the board. The Audit Committee is charged with the following responsibilities:

- To hire, insure compensation for and oversee the work of the foundation's outside auditor.

- To require that a new audit review partner be assigned to the foundation at least every five years.

- To meet with the outside auditor either in person or via conference call before the audit to understand any changes in procedures and to instruct the auditors of any concerns or policy issues of the committee.

- To insure that the auditor of the books is not the firm who does the bookkeeping for the foundation.

- To meet with the outside auditor without staff present after the audit has been completed.

- To make it clear that it wants to hear about any questionable practices or policies within the organization, even if they do not rise to the level of reportable condition under the accounting rules.

- To review the 990-PF to insure its accuracy. This can be accomplished by having the foundation attorney review the 990-PF before it is submitted.

- To review and approve any non-audit services to be performed by the outside auditor.

- To insure that any staff or trustee who may report suspicious activities to the committee or any of its members, shall not be punished for such action and that all such reports shall be investigated by the committee and fixed or justify why corrections are not necessary.

- To present the final Audit Report to the full Board of Trustees for their review and acceptance.

PART II: ETHICS AND ACCOUNTABILITY

We have a governing board that establishes the mission, guides the operations, oversees the effectiveness and ensures the ethical conduct of the foundation. Authority is vested in the governing board as a whole, and each member is equipped to advance the foundation's mission. We consider multiple strategies to further our mission. Our governing board exercises active fiscal oversight. **We recognize and act upon our obligations to multiple stakeholders: the donor and the donor's family, grantees and grantseekers, the public and governmental bodies.** We respect our nonprofit partners' missions and expertise and strive for relationships based on candor, understanding and fairness. We welcome public interest and communicate openly. **Our governing board respects donor intent and later generations' interests while also considering the demands of a changing world.** We plan for family leadership continuity. We have a governing board that establishes the mission, guides the operations, oversees the effectiveness and ensures the ethical conduct of the foundation. Authority is vested in the governing board as a whole, and each member is equipped to advance the foundation's mission. **We consider multiple strategies to further our mission.** Our governing board exercises active fiscal oversight. We recognize and act upon our obligations to multiple stakeholders: the donor and the donor's family, grantees and grantseekers, the public and governmental bodies. **We respect our nonprofit partners' missions and expertise and strive for relationships based on candor, understanding and fairness.** We welcome public interest and communicate openly. Our governing board respects donor intent and later generations' interests while also considering the demands of a changing world. We plan for family leadership continuity. **We have a governing board that establishes the mission, guides the operations, oversees the effectiveness and ensures the ethical conduct of the foundation.** Authority is vested in the governing board as a whole, and each member is equipped to advance the foundation's mission. We consider multiple strategies to further our mission. **Our governing board exercises active fiscal oversight.** We recognize and act upon our obligations to multiple stakeholders: the donor and the donor's family, grantees and grantseekers, the public and governmental bodies. We respect our nonprofit partners' missions and expertise and strive for relationships based on candor, understanding and fairness. **We welcome public interest and communicate openly.** Our governing board respects donor intent and later generations' interests while also considering the demands of a changing world. **We plan for family leadership continuity.** We have a governing board that establishes the mission, guides the operations, oversees the effectiveness and ensures the ethical conduct of the foundation. **Authority is vested in the governing board as a whole, and each member is equipped to advance the foundation's mission.** We consider multiple strategies to further our mission. Our governing board exercises active fiscal oversight. We recognize and act upon our obligations to multiple stake

CHAPTER 5
Respect the Law and Ethical Standards

PRINCIPLE V:

WE RECOGNIZE AND ACT UPON OUR OBLIGATIONS TO MULTIPLE STAKEHOLDERS: THE DONOR AND THE DONOR'S FAMILY, GRANTEES AND GRANTSEEKERS, THE PUBLIC AND GOVERNMENTAL BODIES.

Recognize and act upon your obligations to multiple stakeholders: the donor and the donor's family, grantees and grantseekers, the public and governmental bodies.

When a donor establishes a foundation, the assets of the foundation no longer belong to the donor or the family and may not be used for personal purposes. In return for certain tax benefits from the government, the foundation's assets must be used for charitable purposes.

Because the law provides a tax exemption and other privileges, the government and the public have a right to expect that foundations conduct themselves in an ethical manner. Foundations can show their respect for the public by operating transparently and ethically, preventing fraud and other abuses, and serving the purpose for which they have been created.

As a member of the board, you are a steward of the foundation's assets—responsible for using those assets for charitable purposes and in compliance with the law. You work to fulfill the foundation's mission and to operate under the highest ethical standards. You recognize and treat your foundation's many stakeholders respectfully—including the donor, grantees and grantseekers, the public and the government.

To fulfill your fiduciary duties, you must first know the law. Second, you should create and enforce ethical policies in areas *where there is no law*. This chapter will walk you through the laws on self-dealing, and explain other important foundation policies, as well as ethical issues you might consider.

IN THIS CHAPTER

- Comply with self-dealing rules
- Develop a conflict-of-interest policy
- Embrace diversity
- Create a code of ethics
- Develop and enforce a whistleblower protection policy.

PRACTICE OPTIONS FOR PRINCIPLE V

A. KEEP ABREAST OF THE SELF-DEALING LAWS; AVOID SELF-DEALING AND EVEN THE APPEARANCE OF SELF-DEALING.

Self-dealing laws are among the most difficult for family foundations and their board to understand and follow. Routinely revisit these laws and consult with your foundation's attorney whenever you have a question about self-dealing.

What is self-dealing? By definition, self-dealing is a financial transaction between family foundations and disqualified persons such as board members and trustees (definition below). Self-dealing transactions are prohibited by federal tax law. Here are a few examples of self-dealing activities between a foundation and a disqualified person:

- Lending money or extending credit.

- Furnishing goods, services or activities (this includes renting office space from a disqualified person).

- Selling, exchanging or leasing property (including stationery, design, printing, supplies or insurance).

The main exception to the prohibition against self-dealing: It is permissible to pay reasonable compensation for "personal services" such as legal or accounting assistance that are necessary for the operation of the foundation. Note that the IRS definition of what counts as a personal service is limited (only legal, accounting and investment management services are explicitly included in the definition). Reasonable compensation, put simply, is the amount similar persons are paid for similar work at similar organizations. Some ways to determine reasonable compensation include checking with other foundations in your region of a similar size and assets to compare what they pay for personal services, using salary and other surveys to benchmark compensation and issuing requests for proposals.

However, doing business with a board member raises other issues. Does it send a message to the community that the foundation prefers to do business with those who have connections? How do you deal with a board member who is compensated for personal services if those services prove not of acceptable quality? Does doing business with board members limit opportunities for practicing diversity with foundation vendors? These questions should be discussed by the board before formulating a policy.

People who are considered "disqualified persons" under the tax code include the following:

- Officers, directors or trustees of the foundation.

- Employees with authority to act on behalf of the foundation such as an executive director.

- A substantial contributor to the foundation (individual or corporate).

- Companies or partnerships owned substantially by disqualified persons.

- The family members of all the above. Specifically, the ancestors, spouse, children, grandchildren, great grandchildren, and the spouses of children, grandchildren and great grandchildren. (The brothers and sisters are of disqualified persons are not disqualified persons themselves.)

It's important to educate all disqualified persons involved with the foundation about what is—and what is not—allowed. In many family foundations, there are often disqualified persons who do *not* serve on the board, yet still need to know the rules. For example, family members need to understand that a personal pledge they make to an organization is just that—a personal pledge. The foundation may not pay a pledge on behalf of a family member.

Consider ways to inform the board about the self-dealing rules. For example, you might give disqualified persons a copy of the booklet *Top Ten Ways Family Foundations Get Into Trouble*, Second Edition, (Council on Foundations, 2004). Also consider ways to share information about the self-dealing rules with other disqualified persons involved with the foundation. For example, you might include the rules on self-dealing in a family newsletter or in information provided in an orientation for advisory committee members.

The self-dealing rules are not intuitive. In some situations self-dealing may occur even if a transaction benefits the foundation. For this reason, when it comes to self-dealing, it's better to err on the side of caution. Always ask for legal counsel in situations where there might be self-dealing—or even the appearance of self-dealing. For more information, read *Family Foundations and the Law: What You Need to Know*, Third Edition, Council on Foundations, 2002, by John A. Edie.

Self-dealing: Situations to Avoid

- **Personal family pledges**—A legally binding pledge is a personal debt, and if a disqualified person makes such a pledge, it's an act of self-dealing for a foundation to pay that debt.

- **Attending fundraisers**—If the foundation buys a ticket to a fundraising event and the ticket price includes payment for goods and services (dinner and entertainment), the ticket cannot be used by a disqualified person except as discussed above in "Can You Attend Fundraisers?"

- **Hiring family members as staff**—You can hire a family member as staff and pay them a salary or fee, but the compensation must be reasonable, the services necessary and personal (legal, accounting, banking, investment, etc.), and charitable.

- **Paying travel expenses for family**—The assets of a family foundation generally cannot be used to finance the travel (or any other expense) of spouses and children unless such reimbursement is reported as income on the board member's Form 1099 or W-2 and the member's compensation inclusive of the travel is reasonable OR if the spouse or child have formal, legitimate and meaningful duties serving the foundation.

- **Payment to government officials**—Any agreement to make any payment to a government official is an act of self-dealing unless it is an offer of employment to begin after the official terminates government service.

- **Renting space from a family member**—The payment of rent to any disqualified person by the foundation is self-dealing, even if the rent charged is significantly below market rate and benefits the foundation. However, if the foundation leases space from a disqualified person and the rent is zero, there is no self-dealing.

Excerpts are taken from Top Ten Ways Family Foundations Get Into Trouble, *Second Edition, by Ellen Bryson and John A. Edie, Council on Foundations.*

B. EDUCATE THE GOVERNING BOARD AND STAFF (IF ANY) AS TO WHAT CONSTITUTES CONFLICT OF INTEREST.

Conflicts of interest can be common in the course of foundation business. A conflict occurs when a board or staff member's outside involvements (such as business interests, family relationships, political affiliations or other charitable activities) may make it impossible for him or her to remain unbiased. Most conflicts of interest involve a circumstance where a board or staff member is in a position to benefit from the foundation in a personal, direct or economic way.

A conflict of interest policy provides a roadmap for a foundation in handling a conflict of interest. It helps your board and staff maintain ethical integrity in their decisionmaking and uphold the foundation's reputation. Some examples of conflicts of interest include (but are not limited to):

- A trustee or family member serves as a board member, employee or contractor of an applicant organization or grantee (see note below).

- The foundation hires one of its board members to perform a second, paid role for the foundation, such as an accountant, attorney or investment manager.

- A board member takes part in a decision that could bring personal gain.

Note that in some of the above examples, the foundation's activity is legal but following a conflicts-of-interest policy will help ensure that any decisions are made in the best interest of the foundation. For example, it's perfectly acceptable—and in some foundations, even encouraged—for a trustee or family member to serve on the board of an applicant organization or grantee. (Because opinions vary on this matter, this needs to be an active discussion among your board when developing your conflict-of-interest policy.) What makes a conflict of interest problematic is when the conflict is not revealed, and individual trustees or staff take part in decisions that could personally benefit them.

Because trustees and staff are likely to be affiliated with many organizations in their communities, both on a professional and personal basis, it is natural for conflicts to occur. What's important is how your board or staff handles them when they do.

Your board should take two steps to prepare for such situations:

1. Establish a written conflict of interest policy that identifies types of conduct or transactions that raise concern and that describes how conflicts or perceived conflicts of interest are resolved.

2. Review the conflicts of interest policy with board members, committee members and staff at least annually and document the affiliations or involvement of board members, staff, committee members and their families with potential grantees or foundation service providers, even if the affiliation creates no financial conflict of interest. All individuals should have the responsibility of updating their disclosures as relationships change.

As part of these two steps, the foundation should require that:

- Board members, staff and volunteers disclose the connections, if any, they or their immediate family have to any organization or person that the board is considering for involvement in foundation activities. Common involvements might include business interests, family relationships, political affiliations, and volunteer or other charitable activities. Again, it's common to have these connections, especially in smaller communities. What matters is that you disclose them to the board, and that the board follows its conflict-of-interest policy.

- Board members and staff withdraw from voting on, and perhaps even participating in the discussion of, decisions that present a potential conflict. For example, if you serve on the board of a nonprofit, you might excuse yourself from discussing and voting whether the organization will be awarded a grant (or you might participate in the discussion so that you can give information on the charity but recuse yourself from the vote).

- For every significant transaction, the foundation collects competitive bids to ensure a fair price;

- For each conflict or potential conflict that arises, the board and staff keep a record of the action taken.

Each trustee and staff member should sign the policy document annually, and the board should review and, if necessary, update the policy each year.

At the Americana Foundation, trustees disclose all conflicts of interest at their first meeting in February. Each trustee is given a copy of the complete set and the originals are attached to the permanent minutes.

"It has worked well in that trustees acknowledge any relationship to firms with whom we do business and with existing and potential grantees," said Marlene Fluharty, executive director, Americana Foundation. "This makes it possible to document all potential conflicts upfront and handle them appropriately should one arise."

What happens when a potential conflict results in action that is not illegal, but may be perceived as unethical or just plain inappropriate?

When there is no financial or legal conflict, yet the foundation enters into a transaction—such as awarding a grant—that could be questionable because of conflicting interests, it is sometimes referred to as a "duality of interest." Above, you read the example of a trustee serving on the board of a grant applicant organization. Under the Tax Code, a grant to the organization would generally not create a legal problem. Nonetheless, a situation like this can prompt many questions: *Would the board consider it a conflict to make a grant to the organization? What happens when the board discusses that particular organization? When the topic arises, should the trustee leave the boardroom right away? Or discuss the organization with the board, but abstain from voting?*

"Family foundation board members need to have a serious dialogue about what constitutes a conflict—even beyond the legal minimum. There is no one right answer, but each board should understand what is right for them and their foundation."

—Rob Mayer, trustee, The Nathan Cummings Foundation

There are many views on this topic. For example, in a family foundation survey taken by the Council in 2000, 39 percent of respondents described the situation of trustees who volunteered or served on the boards of grantees as "mutually beneficial"; 49 percent said it was a "dual interest that should be known by the whole board"; and 6 percent called it a "conflict of interest." As you can see by the data, opinions vary among foundations. The answer often depends on the values and culture of your own foundation.

This, however, is just one example of many that your board should discuss and develop procedures for how to handle. Consider the following scenarios and whether they would be a conflict in your board's view:

- An individual board or staff member of the foundation takes or accepts personal recognition, either in public at an event, or in a written publication, for a grant made by the foundation.

- The foundation makes a grant to an organization under circumstances in which the foundation could be accused of trying to use influence for the personal ends of board members—such as a grant to a university where a board member's child has a pending application.

- A board member or family member invests their own assets, along with those of the foundation, to take advantage of a better commission or return—using their position for personal gain.

- A foundation member votes to make a grant to an organization on whose board they serve.

Conflict? Appearance of conflict? Not a problem?

The examples above give your board a start at identifying potential situations, so that you can address them in your conflict-of-interest policy. This policy is not one you want to rush—but one that requires serious dialogue, and planning ahead, on the part of your board. This policy should take into account not only your legal responsibilities—including avoidance of self-dealing transactions—but also your ethical responsibilities.

For more ethical questions like the above, read *Ethical Choices for Family Foundations*, Institute for Global Ethics, or *Responsible Family Philanthropy: A Resource Book for Ethical Decisionmaking for Family Foundations*. See the Resources section at the end of this chapter for information.

For more information on conflicts of interest, read the articles on the Council's Legal Services website under "Foundation Management Legal Resources," at www.cof.org. Recommended articles include "Tread Carefully When Sharing Board Members with Grantseekers."

C. INCORPORATE DIVERSE PEOPLE, PERSPECTIVES, KNOWLEDGE AND EXPERIENCE INTO YOUR WORK.

Family foundations should incorporate a wide array of people, experience, knowledge and skills into their work. Whether bringing diversity to the board or the staff, or by choosing diverse grantees, boards can improve the quality of their grant-making—and their capacity to think creatively.

Diversity can help your foundation in many ways. It:

- Demonstrates accountability and a connection to the broader community.
- Strengthens grantmaking by helping the foundation understand and respond to the groups seeking grants.
- Broadens perspective on the economic, political and/or social problems the foundation is working to resolve.
- Breeds varying opinions, approaches, attitudes and solutions.
- Brings innovation and creative thinking.
- Sets an example for others in the foundation and in the community.

The Jessie Smith Noyes Foundation is one that knows the rewards—and the challenges—of diversity. As President Vic De Luca of the Jessie Smith Noyes Foundation said, "It's critical to have diverse staff, board and grantees. It reflects the real world and it makes us more sensitive to various perspectives.

"We work really hard at trying to create a broad enough pool to attract diverse board and staff members. That's a practice that a lot of foundations say they can't do. My answer is: You just have to do it. You have to go outside your normal circle for recruitment and interview more people than you normally do. For example, you might interview six people for a position, instead of three." Noyes recommends term limits for the board, as they get the board thinking about turnover. He also suggests using a pool of past grantees as a potential source for new board members.

> *"Today we know we are immeasurably better off for having extended the family and have accomplished far more than we could have ever done. We need diversity not simply to reflect the movements we fund, but to understand them."*
>
> *—Edith Muma, trustee, Jessie Smith Noyes Foundation*

But what if your board prefers to stay all family at this time, and/or it has only one or few staff? Even if this is the case, consider these ideas to bring diversity into your work.

1. **Access pertinent data, e.g., censuses, regional indicators and studies** to understand the scope of issues. This will help you learn about your community's demographics and its needs.

2. **Include subject matter experts or community representatives as speakers at board meetings, on committees or on advisory groups** to gain additional knowledge and perspectives. This can be a great way to bring different views to the board—especially if your board is all, or mostly, family members.

3. **Appoint board members and employ staff members who demonstrate the capacity to understand issues and communicate skillfully across cultural, socioeconomic and other boundaries.** This will create a board and work force that can interact successfully with a diverse society and nonprofit world. A word of caution, though: When aiming for a diverse mixture on the board or staff, be sure to choose people based on their experience, skills and community knowledge—*not* just because they fill a demographic slot. No one wants to be a token. Be sure to empower all members equally.

4. **Encourage board and staff to be actively involved in the community (bearing in mind potential conflicts of interest) and to bring new and under-represented perspectives back to the foundation.** Routinely invite members from the community to speak at board meetings. Make site visits. Attend workshops and conferences held by different groups in the community and report back to the board on your findings. To contact with the Council's affinity groups, visit www.cof.org?Affinity.

5. **Establish governance policies and operational and grantmaking practices** to assure implementation throughout the foundation. Consider writing a statement of inclusiveness reflecting the community's demographics,

and how the foundation intends to work with different groups, taking into consideration the many dimensions of diversity including:

- Age/generational
- Gender
- Ethnicity
- Socioeconomic background
- Geography
- Sexual Orientation
- Skill sets
- Profession/occupation.

6. **Develop training resources that promote inclusion and reduce discrimination,** so that the board and staff are well informed on this topic. You might consider asking an outside consultant to train the board and staff on diversity. In addition, look for diversity training at field conferences. Contact the Council's Diversity Programs staff or visit www.cof.org.

Finally, remind the board that by including more diversity in its work, the foundation will enjoy new energy, new ideas and a richness of opinion. Diversity can lead to better discussions—and even better decisions.

In Their Own Words

Why Diversity?

"We don't know all the answers about diversity. But we do know that it's worked for us. More than 50 years after Charles F. Noyes established the Jessie Smith Noyes Foundation in memory of his wife, more of our 16 trustees are from outside the family. Today, the board and staff are male and female, black, white, Latina, Native American and Asian, married and single, and straight and gay. They live in the New York City region and across the country in rural, urban and suburban communities.

"Achieving and maintaining such diversity has not been easy. But it has been essential to pursuing our mission as a foundation. Prior to bringing on board members and staff of color, we had little real knowledge about environmental justice and talked about it even less. Now it's a thread that runs through our grantmaking.

"The changes we made took more than a decade and a half and would have taken longer if we had not pushed ourselves to make them happen sooner. We knew that we needed to augment our skills and our view of how all people connect with the environment, with society and with one another. We don't intend to go back.

"Today, diversity is less the thing we struggle to create and more the air we breathe. It has helped us renew our commitment to work for social, environmental, economic and political justice, and to use our power more strategically."

—From the Jessie Smith Noyes Foundation Diversity Brochure

D. Identify and Practice the Elements of Ethical Conduct.

In philanthropy, you confront a host of challenges: accountability, donor intent, conflicts of interest, financial oversight, confidentiality and more. The desire to operate transparently and the potential of public scrutiny add even more responsibility and can make your choices seem even tougher. How can you make your choices clearly and confidently, based on values and high standards?

The answer lies in your foundation's ethics. Ethics are sometimes defined as "obedience to the unenforceable"; that is, what we do when no clear law or rule exists.

Your foundation should identify, agree upon—and practice—your own ethical standards. By doing so, you build a climate of ethical decisionmaking that helps everyone in the foundation understand the shared, core values—and how to resolve difficult, values-based questions.

By instilling ethics into your work, you not only help your own foundation, but also the entire foundation field. Consider this: When there are abuses by members of the field, Congress and state legislatures enact new laws or regulations to create an enforceable standard. In philanthropy, the laws forbidding self-dealing and mandating a minimum payout rate are examples of what can happen when the public's opinion of foundations erodes. These laws were a response to perceived abuses by foundation trustees.

When you follow a code of ethics, you demonstrate to lawmakers and the public that foundations *can* and *do* regulate themselves and their actions. Toward that end, national associations such as the Council on Foundations and Independent Sector urge foundations and all nonprofits to adopt a code of ethics that guides their governance and operations.

How do you develop a code for your foundation? A code of ethics may include statements on:

- Personal and professional integrity and conduct.
- Mission.
- Governance.
- Conflict of interest.
- Legal compliance.
- Responsible stewardship of resources and financial oversight.
- Openness and disclosure.
- Program evaluation.
- Inclusiveness and diversity.
- Confidentiality.
- Integrity in grantmaking.

Peer Practices

Code of Ethics Builds Understanding

The Dyson Foundation adopted a code of ethics after the founder died, and the foundation began to grow quickly as a result of becoming fully funded through his estate. Dyson staff developed it after reviewing similar policies from other family foundations. "A code of ethics gives everyone, board and staff, a common basis for understanding the values of the foundation," said executive vice president Diana Gurieva.

The code is posted on the foundation's website for all to see. "We feel that it enunciates certain values that are important to the foundation, such as fairness, open-mindedness and the fact that we do not pay our board compensation for their service," said Gurieva.

A code of ethics will help your foundation demonstrate its accountability, values and transparency. Your board should create and oversee the code. To do so, you might convene an ad hoc committee to determine what your code should include.

For foundations that have already adopted a code of ethics, work with your board and staff (and particularly new board members and staff) to review it regularly, and ensure that you have a process in place for adhering to the code.

See samples at the end of this chapter. To customize your own code of ethics, visit www.independentsector.org. You can find more about ethical decisionmaking at www.foundationethics.org, a site developed for foundations by the Institute on Global Ethics (www.globalethics.org).

Excerpts of the above taken from Grantmaking Basics II: A Field Guide for Funders, *Council on Foundations, 2004, www.cof.org.*

E. Develop a policy to handle good-faith complaints about violations of foundation policy or the conduct of foundation board or staff.

In addition to a Code of Ethics, your foundation should develop a policy to handle good-faith complaints about violations of foundation policy or the conduct of foundation board or staff. This recommendation comes in the wake of recent corporate scandals and the new laws that affect for-profit organizations. Although there is no law at this time that requires nonprofit organizations to have such a policy, it is a best practice for foundations to adopt one.

Such a policy is known as a "whistleblower policy." A whistleblower policy protects individuals who come forward with credible information on illegal practices, or violations of adopted policies, of an organization.

"But I'm a small family foundation," you might say. "Do we really need a whistleblower policy?"

In this case, size doesn't matter. According to recent recommendations by the Panel on the Nonprofit Sector (www.nonprofitpanel.org), an independent effort by charities and foundations to improve nonprofit oversight and governance, *all* charitable organizations, regardless of size, should adopt and enforce such a policy.

In a written policy, you board should explicitly state how and to whom trustees and staff should report a complaint or matter of concern. The process must ensure confidentiality and protection for anyone reporting issues or concerns, so people who potentially "blow the whistle" feel safe from retaliation— meaning any kind of punishment, firing, demotion, harassment or discrimination.

When you are ready to develop a policy of this type, the following components are common:

- General standard of conduct
- Wrong conduct definition
- Reporting responsibility
- Statement of no retaliation

- Violations reported to designated person
- Good faith
- Confidentiality
- Ways to handle reported wrongful conduct.

As a part of your policy, you will want to explain the reporting procedures. Procedures at foundations may differ, depending on your size and culture.

At a smaller foundation, for example, your policy might be carried out in a straightforward way. The board might designate one or two people (who are trusted and can be contacted relatively easily) as the receivers of the complaints. These people must pledge to an appropriate level of confidentiality in this position. In your foundation's policies and procedures handbook, you should state that "all concerns go to the designated persons for investigation, and retaliation is not allowed."

Larger foundations might choose to have a more formal process, such as hiring an outside ombudsman to handle complaints. For example, one foundation has implemented their policy by contracting with an outside organization that operates 24 hours a day, seven days a week, to receive confidential telephone calls to report unethical or illegal activities. The organization confidentially reports this information to a member of the foundation's board, where it can be appropriately addressed. Other options include reporting to the board chair, the foundation's outside counsel or the chair of a governance or executive committee.

Regardless of your foundation's process, it's a good idea to remind everyone periodically that the policy exists. Send a memo or e-mail message to the board and staff or include it in the foundation's newsletter or other internal publication.

For more information, visit the National Council for Nonprofit Associations at www.ncna.org or Nonprofit Risk Management Center at www.nonprofitrisk.org.

In sum, ask yourself:

- Do my fellow board members and I understand and comply with the self-dealing laws?

- How does our foundation identify and deal with possible conflicts of interest?

- How do we encourage diverse viewpoints in our work and include the expertise we need?

- How do we ensure adherence to our code of ethics?

- Do we have a means to handle concerns about our foundation's practices and personnel?

Resources

Family Foundations and the Law: What You Need to Know, Third Edition. By John A. Edie. Council on Foundations, 2002. Visit www.cof.org.

Legal Essentials for Small Foundations. Association of Small Foundations, 2005. Visit www.smallfoundations.org.

Policymaking Made Clear: Eleven Foundation Policies Your Board Should Consider. By Elaine Gast. Association of Small Foundations, 2005. Visit www.smallfoundations.org.

Responsible Family Philanthropy: A Resource Book for Ethical Decisionmaking for Family Foundations. By Michael Rion. Council on Foundation, 1998. Visit www.cof.org/publications.

Top Ten Ways Family Foundations Get Into Trouble, Second Edition. By Ellen Bryson and John A. Edie. Council on Foundations, 2004. Item #849. Visit www.cof.org/publications.

What Foundation Boards Are Saying about Diversity. By Ellen Bryson and Steve Parsons. Council on Foundations, 2003. Visit www.cof.org/publications.

SAMPLE DOCUMENTS FOR PRINCIPLE V

Sample Conflict-of-Interest Policy
Courtesy of the James Irvine Foundation

Purpose of the Statement of Policy. The James Irvine Foundation is committed to integrity and fairness in the conduct of all of its activities. Inevitably, the interests of Directors and employees will involve them in organizations, causes and other endeavors which intersect with the affairs of the Foundation. It would disadvantage the Foundation to deprive it of the involvement of interested colleagues, but their participation in Foundation decision making cannot impair the fairness and integrity of Foundation processes. This statement of principle is intended to further the work of the Foundation by facilitating the substantive contributions of its employees and Directors through providing for disclosure of other interests and by requiring abstention from decision-making actions which affect non-Foundation affiliations or interests. In addition, the Foundation would suffer if there were any appearance of bias or self-interest in its activities. These principles are intended, as well, to preclude any such appearance.

This statement is not a codification of rules of conduct; rather it is an expression of intention and purpose which should be interpreted and applied to achieve its stated objective. Individuals worthy of affiliation with the Foundation will govern themselves by that spirit.

Disclosure. Directors and employees of the Foundation are committed to communicating fully with the Foundation regarding any relationship or commitment which could affect the impartial fulfillment of their role in the affairs of the Foundation. This policy refers to such a relationship or commitment as affiliation. Affiliation may be defined as the close involvement with a vendor, service provider, or grantee on the part of (a) a director of the Foundation, (b) a staff member of the Foundation, or (c) the spouse or equivalent, parents, or children of a director or staff member. Affiliation includes, but is not limited to, serving as a board member, employee, or consultant to a current or potential grantee, service provider, or vendor, or doing business with the grantee, service provider, or vendor. Antecedent affiliations and indirect associations also warrant disclosure. In principle, extra-Foundation affiliations or interests should be disclosed to other participants in the Foundation's decision-making process whenever there is any doubt about whether disclosure is required.

Disclosures ordinarily should be made to the President by members of the staff and to the Chair of the Board by other members of the Board of Directors. A report of board member affiliations will be compiled and provided to board members in the current year's Board Handbook.

Abstention or Recusal from Foundation Decision Making. In all situations in which disclosure of affiliation should be made, the board or staff member should either abstain or recuse himself or herself from decision-making actions. Where the action involves the consideration of a grant recommendation at a board meeting, the affiliated board member should formally recuse himself or herself, and discussion of the proposed grant recommendation should occur without the affiliated board or staff member. Where the action involves ratification of a previously approved grant, the affiliated individual should abstain from the ratifying action, and the abstention should be formally noted in the Foundation's minutes. It is important to note that the Foundation believes that its work will be furthered by the willingness of board and staff to share information of bearing upon the matter under consideration, and such participation is encouraged, provided appropriate disclosure of affiliation has been made to other participants.

No Return Benefit. In considering any decision regarding an organization or person with which a Foundation employee or Director is affiliated, the Foundation shall avoid any transaction which results in any direct or indirect economic benefit to the affiliated person or which would constitute self-dealing under Internal Revenue Code Section 4941. Incidental and tenuous benefits to affiliated persons, such as name recognition or public acknowledgment, are permitted.

Avoid the Appearance of Conflict. While the substance of integrity is the essence of the Foundation's approach to these matters, avoiding the appearance of conflict is an important collateral objective. To that end, the Foundation will not customarily make grants to, or contract with, organizations which employ affiliated persons. The President, with the concurrence of the Chair of the Board of Directors, may approve exceptions to this policy when the work of the Foundation will be furthered thereby or where the grant or contract will not affect the job or compensation of the affiliated person in question.

No significant personal benefit of any nature may be derived by any affiliated person from any such organization.

Adopted by the Board of Directors, May 23, 1994
Revised, June 15, 2004

Sample Conflict-of-Interest Policy

Courtesy of the Wallace Alexander Gerbode Foundation

The board and staff members of the Wallace Alexander Gerbode Foundation are encouraged to play active roles in their communities by serving as board members or otherwise being involved with a wide spectrum of nonprofit organizations. This means that, from time to time, potential conflicts of interest or the appearance of such conflicts will inevitably arise. It is the Foundation's policy to deal with such conflicts in as open and appropriate a way as possible.

Conflicting involvements include but are not limited to the following: Foundation board or staff members serving as board members of applicant organizations, immediate family members of Foundation board or staff members serving as board members of applicant organizations, Foundation board members or staff members or their immediate family members being employed by or doing business with applicant organizations.

In case of such conflicts or the appearance thereof, Foundation board members and staff are expected to disclose the conflict prior to making any related grant decisions. Once such a disclosure has been made, the remaining board members will determine whether or not there is a potential conflict of interest. Should it be so considered, the board member involved shall abstain from voting and shall not participate in the discussion of the applicant organization other than to answer specific questions that may be raised by other board members.

In cases where the Foundation's board of trustees decides to award a grant to an organization and one or more of the Foundation's board members has abstained from voting as the result of a conflict or the appearance thereof or a staff member has a conflict or the appearance thereof, such grants and board or staff members shall be identified in the Foundation's annual report.

Sample Diversity Statements
Courtesy of the Nathan Cummings Foundation

Statement in our personnel manual:

The Foundation strictly prohibits discrimination against any employee or applicant for employment because of the individual's race, color, sex, religion, national origin, age, sexual orientation, disability, political affiliation, veteran status, genetic predisposition or carrier status, marital status or any other characteristic protected by law. This policy applies to all Foundation activities, including but not limited to, recruitment, hiring, compensation, assignment, training, promotion, discipline and discharge. As detailed below, this policy also bans discriminatory harassment.

The Foundation will provide reasonable accommodation consistent with the law to otherwise qualified employees and prospective employees with a disability and to employees and prospective employees with needs related to their religious observance or practices. What constitutes a reasonable accommodation depends on the circumstances and thus will be addressed by the Foundation on a case-by-case basis.

Statement is in our job announcements:

The Foundation values and is committed to diversity on its staff. It therefore invites nominations and applications without regard to race, ethnicity, gender, physical disability or sexual orientation.

Commitment to diversity statement in our general grant applications:

The foundation supports organizations that employ, compensate and advance personnel without regard to sex, race, color, religion, age, national origin, veteran status, physical disability, sexual orientation or marital status. Please include information on the composition of your organization's board and staff and describe your organization's commitment to diversity.

This statement is in the guidelines for Trustee searches:

The Board is committed to diversity in the Foundation's programs and its own composition, and affirmatively seeks to add people of color and women to the Board.

Sample Conflict of Interest Statement

Courtesy of the Americana Foundation

A possible conflict of interest could arise in any situation in which the Americana Foundation has business or financial dealings with a Member of the Board of Trustees individually or with a corporation, partnership or other business enterprise of which the Trustee and/or a member of the Trustee's immediate family is an officer, direct partner or substantial stockholder. A possible conflict of interest could also arise in connection with a decision to make a grant to a tax-exempt, not-for-profit organization of which the Trustee is an officer, director or trustee.

Each Trustee of the Foundation, by written instrument delivered annually to the Executive Director, will disclose the corporations, partnerships, proprietorships and other business enterprises of which the Trustee or member of the Trustee's immediate family is an officer, director, partner or substantial stockholder or owner and which might reasonably be expected to have business or financial dealings with the Americana Foundation.

When any possible conflict of interest of any Trustee becomes relevant to the making of a grant or to any matter requiring action of the Board, the Trustee shall call it to the attention of the Board, shall not vote on such matter, and shall not attempt to exert personal influence in connection therewith. Any Trustee who is excluded from voting because of such possible conflict of interest may briefly state their position in the matter and answer pertinent questions from other Trustees when the Trustee's knowledge of the matter will assist the Board in its deliberations.

Connections with Grant Recipients

Trustees and staff are encouraged to expand their levels of public service by serving on *pro bono publico* boards and committees. There is however, the potential for perceived conflict of interest when the organization is a potential or existing grantee of the foundation. It is therefore the policy of the Americana Foundation that Trustees and staff will acknowledge membership on Boards and committees when filing the annual Conflict of Interest forms and shall declare any such membership during grant request discussions and decisions. The affected Trustee shall not vote on such matters and shall not attempt to exert personal influence in connection therewith. Staff shall not make recommendations on grant requests submitted when the staff person serves as a Board or Committee member of that organization. Staff does not vote on matters of the foundation but may respond to questions posed by the Trustees during any grant discussions provided there is no attempt to exert personal influence in connection with the voting.

I, _____, a trustee of the Americana Foundation acknowledge that I have received, understand and have agreed with that the preceding conflict of interest policy of the Americana Foundation and that it is to be adhered to through all actions of the board and staff. In addition, I will insure that all actions of the foundation will comply with applicable state and federal rules and regulations.

Signature:_____

Date:_____

Sample Conflict of Interest Disclosure Form

Courtesy of the Americana Foundation

I,_____, Trustee of the Americana Foundation do hereby disclose the following corporations, partnerships, proprietorships and other business enterprises of which I or members of my immediate family is an officer, director, partner, or substantial stockholder or owner and which have or might reasonably be expected to have business or financial dealings with the Americana Foundation.

I also hereby disclose the following organizations of which I or members of my immediate family am a member or director and which may be a potential or existing grantee of the foundation.

Date:_____

Signature:

Sample Code of Ethics

Courtesy of the Dyson Foundation

The Dyson Foundation seeks to integrate the personal style and flexibility of a family philanthropic endeavor with the best grantmaking practices of the foundation community. With this goal in mind, the following standards have been adopted to guide the trustees, directors, officers and employees in their philanthropic undertakings and in their conduct of all Foundation business.

1. Serving the public interest shall guide all of the Foundation's work, and shall be the basis for board and staff decision-making at all levels of the organization.

2. Everyone will be expected to bring objective thinking, critical analysis and a discerning, empathetic heart to the Foundation's deliberations.

3. Everyone will be tolerant of the ideas and positions of others, and all matters will be approached with an open mind.

4. Decisions and judgments will be based on the most complete and accurate information that is available, and each director will be expected to familiarize him or herself as thoroughly as possible with any information that is disseminated for a meeting.

5. Board directors shall serve without compensation.

6. No director or staff person will use his or her position with the Foundation in a manner that will inure financially to his or her benefit.

7. Decisions of the Foundation's Board of Directors will be made, whenever possible, through a process of consensus. Appropriate discretion is important when discussing the Board's deliberations outside of the confines of meetings. Care should be taken to not damage the reputation of grantees, or to comment on the Foundation's grantmaking process in outside discussions, so as not to stifle the candor and open discussion that the Foundation strives for in its decision-making processes.

8. In order to avoid the appearance or potential of any conflict of interest, board members and staff will disclose, at the earliest possible opportunity, any relationship that they may have with a current or prospective grantee. Such relationships include voluntary service on a board, an employment or a consulting relationship, or similar relationships of immediate family members with a grantee organization. In connection with any action by the Board, this disclosure will be duly recorded in the minutes or other resolutions relating to such actions, and the interested director will abstain from voting on any such action. Directors and staff shall also disclose any material facts as to his or her relationship with any firm, association or other entity that seeks to enter into any other kind of business relationship with the Foundation.

9. Staff and board directors will not accept any gifts, payments or loans from vendors or suppliers of goods or services to the Foundation, or from organizations which have applied to the Foundation for a grant, are current grantees or may likely be applying to the Foundation for a grant in the future.

Adopted by the Board of Directors October 1997
Revised June 2004
Revised October 2004

Sample Code of Ethics

Courtesy of Richard and Susan Smith Family Foundation

Trustees and staff of the Foundation act with honesty, integrity and openness in all their dealings as representatives of the Foundation.

The Foundation has a clearly stated mission and purpose, approved by the Trustees in pursuit of the public good. The Foundation's programs support that mission.

The Foundation establishes and follows clear processes for informing the public about grant opportunities and for receiving, reviewing and acting on grant applications that are consistent with its policies and purposes.

Trustees and staff are aware of their responsibilities of managing the Foundation's assets prudently and responsibly. Appropriate legal and financial management advice is procured and the Foundation spends an adequate amount on administrative expenses to ensure effective accounting systems, internal controls, competent staff, and other expenditures critical to professional management.

All financial reports are factually accurate and complete in all material respects and any forms required by the government are completed accurately by independent accountants and filed in a timely manner.

The Foundation compensates staff, and any others who may receive compensation, in a manner that is reasonable and appropriate.

Trustees and staff and their families will not profit financially from any philanthropic grant or activity or other compensation. There shall be no fees for family Trustees. If a Trustee or staff member has any personal or family affiliation or involvement with any organization for which a grant is considered, that affiliation will be disclosed and noted in the Foundation's meeting minutes, and the Trustee or staff member will be recused from discussion or voting.

Adopted 5/11/04

Sample Whistleblower Policy

Used with permission of the Association of Small Foundations, www.smallfoundations.org

General

The _____Foundation (the "Foundation") expects its directors, officers and employees to observe high standards of business and personal ethics in the conduct of their duties and responsibilities on behalf of the Foundation. As employees and representatives of the Foundation, such directors, officers and employees must practice honesty and integrity in fulfilling their responsibilities and comply with all applicable laws and regulations and all policies of the Foundation. "Wrongful Conduct", as defined in this Policy, of any kind is prohibited.

Reporting Responsibility

It is the responsibility of all directors, officers and employees to report Wrongful Conduct to an appropriate representative of the Foundation in accordance with the provisions of this Policy. "Wrongful Conduct" is any activity in violation of any state, federal or local law or regulation or any Foundation policy undertaken by a director, officer or employee in the performance of such individual's official duties, whether or not such activity is within the scope of his or her intended responsibilities on behalf of the Foundation. This includes, but is not limited to, corruption, malfeasance, bribery, theft, fraud, coercion, conversion, malicious prosecution, harassment, or misuse of the Foundation's property and facilities.

No Retaliation

No director, officer or employee who reports Wrongful Conduct in good faith in accordance with this Policy shall suffer harassment, retaliation or adverse employment consequence. An employee that retaliates against someone who has reported Wrongful Conduct in good faith is subject to discipline up to and including termination of employment. This Policy is intended to encourage and enable employees and others to raise serious concerns with the Foundation.

Directors, officers and employees are also protected against retaliation for providing information to, or otherwise in an investigation by, a regulatory authority or law enforcement agency, any member of Congress or committee of Congress, or any person with supervisory authority over an employee or who has authority to investigate, discover or terminate Wrongful Conduct where such information or investigation relates to any conduct of the Foundation that the reporting individual believes constitutes Wrongful Conduct within the meaning of this Policy. Any director, officer or employee who files, testifies, participates in, or otherwise assists in a proceeding relating to alleged Wrongful Conduct is also protected against retaliation. Acts of retaliation by any director, officer or employee are prohibited.

Reporting Violations

A director, officer or employee who wishes to report Wrongful Conduct is asked to make such report to the _____ or the executive director of the Foundation, who have specific responsibility to investigate all reported Wrongful Conduct. If an investigation substantiates that Wrongful Conduct has taken place, the _____ or the executive director will report such conduct to appropriate personnel and the board of directors. If for some reason a director, officer or employee prefers not to make the report of Wrongful Conduct to the _____ or the executive director, he or she should make such report to any other officer of the Foundation.

Acting in Good Faith

Anyone filing a report concerning a violation or suspected violation of law or other Wrongful Conduct must be acting in good faith and have reasonable cause for believing the information disclosed indicates a violation of law or other Wrongful Conduct. Any allegations that prove not to be substantiated and which prove to have been made maliciously or knowingly to be false will be viewed as a serious disciplinary offense.

Confidentiality

Reports of Wrongful Conduct may be submitted on a confidential basis by the complainant or may be submitted anonymously. Such reports will be kept confidential to the extent possible, consistent with the need to conduct an adequate investigation.

Handling of Reported Wrongful Conduct

The associate-director-finance, the executive director or other officer will notify the individual who has made a report under this Policy of the Foundation's receipt of the report of Wrongful Conduct within five business days of his or her receipt of the report. All reports will be promptly investigated and appropriate corrective action will be taken if warranted by the investigation.

CHAPTER 6
Respect Your Nonprofit Partners

PRINCIPLE VI:

WE RESPECT OUR NONPROFIT PARTNERS' MISSIONS AND EXPERTISE AND STRIVE FOR RELATIONSHIPS BASED ON CANDOR, UNDERSTANDING AND FAIRNESS.

A grant is the highest form of respect that your family foundation can give an organization. It shows that you believe strongly in the nonprofit's mission— so much so that you're willing to provide the financial backing it needs to succeed.

But beyond making the grant award, how can you show nonprofits respect and understanding?

Think in terms of what a nonprofit needs from you.

Grant applicants, for example, need to know two things from you up front: what you fund and how they can apply for a grant. Once they apply for a grant, they need to know you received their proposal and when they can expect to hear back from you.

If you accept their proposal, they need to know when they will receive your funds and what *you* expect from them by way of terms, conditions and reporting requirements. If you decline their proposal, they need a prompt "no" and if appropriate, your reasons why.

Outside of the actual grant application process, nonprofits need to feel that you listen to them and respect their time. They need you to be open, honest and accessible through the grant process and beyond.

IN THIS CHAPTER

- How to craft clear, grantee-friendly guidelines and procedures
- How to conduct respectful site visits
- Tips for improving grantee/grantor relations
- Ways to solicit feedback from grantees and grantseekers
- How to respond to complaints.

The nonprofits in your community are the people on the front lines, working for causes you care about. They are your partners. Without nonprofits, you're just a check writer with no community impact. By taking a few simple steps, you can help the partnerships succeed and gain a better relationship with your grantees in the process. This chapter will show you how.

PRACTICE OPTIONS FOR PRINCIPLE V

A. DEVELOP TRANSPARENT GRANTS MANAGEMENT PROCESSES.

Grantees and grantseekers frequently complain that grants application processes are convoluted and time-consuming. As a part of your application process, you should consider the following:

1. **Create clear and complete program guidelines and application procedures. Consider accepting common grant applications**, making the process simpler and more efficient for grantseekers.

Program Guidelines

Your guidelines and procedures describe your grant program, how it operates, and how and when applicants should apply. It is your way of connecting with nonprofits in your community before you make actual contact. Once you develop guidelines, you should post them online where grantseekers can find them.

Guidelines can be short and simple, as long as they are clear. Many foundations include a description of the following in their grant guidelines:

- Values, vision, mission statement.

- Brief history of the foundation (optional).

- Statement on the nature and size of grants.

- Any restrictions on grants—*What will the foundation fund and not fund?*

- Application process and deadlines—*What should grant seekers send, and in what format? How many pages? Any attachments? To whose attention? When is the deadline?*

- A description of the selection process—*How will proposals be evaluated? How and when will the board make its funding decisions?*

- Any special policies—*What rules, if any, apply for first-time grants, renewals, site visits, grant reporting or evaluation, etc.?*

- Contact information for the foundation—*How should applicants contact the foundation in case they have inquiries?*

Application Procedures

- Rather than accept a full proposal from grantseekers, some foundations prefer a letter of inquiry first. This is a brief letter outlining an organization's activities to determine if there is sufficient interest to warrant submitting a full proposal. Letters of inquiry can save time for both foundation staff and the applicant. Once the foundation reviews letters of inquiry, it can then invite those nonprofits that fall under its guidelines to submit a full proposal. If you ask for a letter of inquiry, be sure to describe the format and what information grantseekers should include. You should also acknowledge receiving all letters of inquiry—not just those that have potential to become a proposal.

- In addition to letters of inquiry, many foundations save grantseekers time by asking for a Common Grant Application (CGA). In many areas of the country, grantmakers have jointly created common application forms. These simple but effective forms make it easier to apply for grants and easier for the foundations to review proposals. The form can help reduce the amount

Online Grant Applications

The Dyson Foundation launched an online eligibility questionnaire and letter of inquiry in March 2004. The questionnaire won't let applicants proceed if their answers don't meet the funding guidelines. As a result, the foundation can devote most of its time to inquiries from applicants that are qualified—a big time saver. "We decided to create an online eligibility questionnaire because we found ourselves getting a great number of proposals that wouldn't fit within our guidelines. This way, we help save our grantseekers time," said Executive Vice President Diana Gurieva.

The online application was part of a $50,000 re-launch of the foundation's website. In four months, the number of applications the foundation received has doubled, but a much larger number fit the guidelines—from less than 50 percent to 80 percent. "Our eligibility questionnaire has been used over 9,000 times–it's the highest-viewed section of our website," said Gurieva.

of time grantseekers must spend rearranging basic information from one proposal to the next to fit grantmakers' varying application requirements. CGAs usually cover one specific geographic region and are almost always developed through a regional association of grantmakers. For examples of CGAs, visit the Forum of Regional Associations at www.givingforum.org.

2. **Request only the information (pre- and post-grant) that will actually be used in decisionmaking and that corresponds appropriately to the size or purpose of the grant.**

   - Be honest: What do you really *need* to see from grantseekers? What is the minimum amount of information that will satisfy your due diligence?

   - Try to spare grantseekers the trouble of developing a lengthy, time-intensive proposal. They don't have time for that and neither do you. Instead, encourage them to share as much as they can about their program, goals and finances in as short a space as possible. Set guidelines and a page limit in your application procedures.

   - You might set different requirements for different grants, depending on the size and scope of the award. For example, for smaller grants, you might only require a three-page application, while for larger grants, you might ask for a full narrative proposal, with the appropriate attachments.

   - Regardless of the method you choose, always be respectful of what you ask of applicants. Consider the amount of time and cost they will spend preparing the proposal.

3. **Specify the steps and timing of the review process.**

   - Put yourself in your grant applicants' shoes. Would you want to be waiting around forever to find out if you got a grant?

   - Be upfront about how your grant process works. Outline the steps in your application procedures and then remind applicants again when you acknowledge receiving their proposal.

   - If the board's deadline for approving grants gets pushed back, send applicants a quick e-mail. Keep them informed as to where the board is in its process and when they can expect to hear from you again.

4. **Acknowledge grantseeker inquiries and submissions promptly.**

   - Be prompt in your response to letters and proposals. The grantseeker likely worked hard to get the proposal in by your deadline. The least that applicants deserve is an acknowledgment that you received it. Make it a habit to respond in less than two weeks—even if you send a pre-formatted postcard or e-mail.

   - If a proposal is clearly ineligible, a quick and simple reply allows the grantseeker more time to try its luck somewhere else. If the proposal *is* eligible and up for consideration, explain your grants review process to applicants, and give them a timeframe in which they can expect to hear from you again.

   For a sample acknowledgment postcard, see the end of this chapter.

5. **Use grant agreement letters to outline mutual expectations.**

   Being clear in your expectations is perhaps the most important part of grantmaking. The best way to do this is through a grant agreement, signed by both parties. A grant agreement outlines your expectations for how the money will be paid and spent, and how the grant results will be reported.

   A good grant agreement will address the following:

   - The amount and purposes of the grant.

   - A payment schedule.

   - The grant reporting and evaluation process.

   - An attached copy of the budget for the project, with a provision that no changes can be made without the foundation's approval.

   - A provision that if the grantee's charitable tax-exempt status is changed or revoked, the foundation will be notified immediately and the grant can be terminated.

   - An agreement that if the grantee organization fails to abide by the terms of the grant agreement, the foundation may terminate the grant and recover any unspent or improperly spent grant funds.

   - If and how the foundation would like the grantee to publicize the grant.

The grant agreement should be signed by a grantee officer, who certifies that he or she has been authorized by the board to execute the contract. The signed copy of the agreement should be returned to your foundation.

It helps to ask grantees if they understand the grant agreement and if they have any questions. Having this conversation at the beginning of a grant can save misunderstandings later.

See sample grant agreements at the end of this chapter.

6. **Explains the rationale for declined grants and gives constructive feedback when appropriate.**

   ■ By the nature of the job, grantmakers must frequently say no to grantseekers. In some cases, grant applicants simply aren't eligible—they don't fall within your grant guidelines or funding area. Other times, they might be an eligible organization with a worthy project, but the foundation doesn't have enough money to go around.

   ■ Regardless, you should notify declined applicants in a timely manner and in writing. You might state that "there is not a match" between the foundation's grantmaking priorities and their program at this time and if appropriate, leave the door open for future contact.

   ■ Depending on your foundation's style and intention, the amount of feedback you give to grantseekers may vary. Some foundations offer constructive criticism in writing or in person. Others aren't comfortable getting so detailed.

   ■ Yet, if you offer applicants no feedback, you might just be inviting another ineligible or inadequate proposal in the future—wasting both the applicant's, and your, time. Here's a tip: Tell them outright whether they should resubmit an amended or new proposal in the future. If they aren't eligible and never will be, tell them so (politely, of course). Although they may be disappointed, they will appreciate your honesty and move on.

   ■ Some foundations direct any questions from declined applicants to the foundation's staff. Often, the staff member will have been outside of the grant decision and therefore can be more objective when giving the grantseeker advice.

In Their Own Words

Saying No Nicely

"Saying 'no' may be very difficult at times, but it is necessary. With limited funds, it simply is not possible to support all deserving, worthwhile programs. Having served as a development officer for nonprofits before moving to the grantmaking side of this philanthropic equation 30 years ago, I feel strongly that direct communication is essential; it saves both sides time, money and effort. Honest, up-front assessments are helpful to all. For example, if there is no chance, tell the inquirer that immediately and clearly. Don't make development or administrative personnel waste their time—instead, encourage them to explore other funding sources."

—Ann D. Gralnek, independent consultant that serves as senior advisor to the George Frederick Jewett Foundation

Giving Advice to Grantseekers

"We offer free technical assistance if we see something that might strengthen a grant applicant's proposal. This isn't to say that we tell them how to run their program, or that they will or won't get a grant if they don't take our suggestion. But we might say something like: 'The board would prefer to see a funder's list with the specific dollar amounts in your proposal,' or something similar. It's always in terms of what the board would prefer, not what we require. We're not shy to tell them what might help them."

—Jane Stamstad, executive director, James R. Thorpe Foundation

B. CONDUCT SITE VISITS WHEN APPROPRIATE, GUIDED BY THE SIZE AND PURPOSE OF THE GRANT AND THE IMPACT ON THE GRANTEE.

Many foundations use site visits as part of their grant application process. In addition to pre-grant site visits, some also make site visits to monitor grants or for post-grant evaluation.

Site visits can be as rewarding as they are informative. By visiting the nonprofit, you gain a greater understanding of its needs and how they fit within your foundation's mission. The visit introduces you to the people actually doing the work—key staff, board members and the people the organization serves. This helps you assess the commitment of those involved and at the same time, demonstrates your foundation's commitment to due diligence.

But site visits also take up an organization's valuable time. Be sure that your site visits are guided by the size and purpose of the grant and consider how the visit will affect the grantee's daily operations.

As an example from the field, the James R. Thorpe Foundation believes in respectful site visits. "At our site visits, we want nonprofits to feel that we respect their time and that we want to learn from them. We tell them exactly what to expect in advance—that we will stay with them for about an hour, or an hour and a half, that we would like a tour and that if possible, we would like to meet with some of the people they serve. We don't want our site visits to remain behind closed doors."

Here are a few tips for thoughtful communication with grantseekers, both before and during a site visit:

- **Schedule the visit well in advance**—Be respectful of the organization's schedule. Ask the grantseeker when would be the best time for the visit, and schedule a meeting that is mutually convenient.

- **Tell them what you want to learn**—Prepare a checklist of questions you would like to address and people you would like to meet; share that list with the organization *before* the visit.

- **Come prepared**—Read the proposal a few times and research the background of the organization.

- **Use their time well**—Set an agenda for the meeting, perhaps including time for introductions, a tour (if appropriate), a brief presentation by the grantseeker, questions and answers and a discussion of the review and approval process. Set a timeframe (usually between one and two hours) and stick to it.

- **Create a nonthreatening tone**—Remember that site visits are conversations—not inspections.

In Their Own Words

Site Visits Give Insight

"We feel it is very important for each of our three-member board to be familiar with our grantee called Mission Honduras. Because it's our largest grantee, it's important for us to go down there and see the operation for ourselves. Site visits give us a feel for the operation, allow us to meet the people and see it as it is. It also gives them a chance to know us, and see that we care about what they do.

"When we are there, we stay at the mission with them, living as they do. This gives us true insight into the lifestyle, the food, the culture—it's a real eye opener. We feel our help would be less effective if we didn't understand what the situation is in Central America."

—Tom Teeling, board secretary and executive director, John & Susan Dewan Foundation

C. ACKNOWLEDGE AND MINIMIZE THE EFFECTS OF THE IMBALANCE OF POWER IN GRANTOR/GRANTEE RELATIONSHIPS.

Let's face it. A grantor/grantee relationship is one based on money. There are the givers and the receivers—making for an inherent, albeit unspoken, inequality between grantor and grantee.

Some nonprofits find it difficult to understand how foundations work. They don't know where the money comes from or how to access the foundation. They might associate foundations with power and authority, and therefore feel intimidated.

The more your foundation acknowledges that grantees might feel this way, the more you can minimize the imbalance—and thereby build a better relationship with the nonprofits you serve.

But how do you do this? The James R. Thorpe Foundation offered some advice. "As a family foundation officer, I am very interested in seeing how we can bridge the chasm between foundations and nonprofits. I think one of the strengths of the family foundation is the opportunity to get up close and personal with the people you serve," said Edith Thorpe, president of the foundation.

One way board members can do this is through personal involvement with grantees—in site visits, for example. According to Jane Stamstad, the Thorpe Foundation funds smaller, grassroots organizations—many of which have never hosted a site visit before. "Before the visit, I talk with the nonprofit, explaining that although we are interested in the organization, the competition is keen—meaning a site visit doesn't automatically mean they're getting a grant," said Stamstad. "We frame the visit as an opportunity for them to inform the larger community—in this case, a family foundation—and make them believe, as we do, that we are novices, there to learn from them."

Another good tip: "At site visits, our board members make sure to dress casually—which also helps remove some of the 'we vs. them' imbalance."

Peer Practices

Warning Grantees of Possible Cutbacks

The Marshall L. and Perrine McCune Charitable Foundation in Santa Fe, New Mexico, works to minimize the imbalance with its grantees through open communication—in good times and in bad. A few years ago, the foundation was affected by the downturn in the economy. In the spirit of openness, the foundation sent letters to all of its grantees advising them to prepare for possible grant cutbacks. "We thought it would only be fair to let grantees know so that as they prepared their budgets for the coming year, they wouldn't have false expectations," said Owen Lopez, executive director. The foundation made it clear that it still encouraged requests and it would honor its multiyear commitments. How did grantees react to the news? According to Lopez, the response was overwhelmingly positive. "We received notes and calls from many of our grantees, thanking us for letting them know in advance."

The Tracy Family Foundation approaches the imbalance in a different way. Three times a year before every funding cycle, the foundation hosts a grant information meeting. All agencies that are applying for a grant are invited to this meeting, at which the foundation gives them information about its different grant programs, where money comes from and more. They even go through the online application with grantseekers to make sure they understand how to submit it. According to Executive Director Jean Buckley, "This process could not be labeled as perfect, but it makes our foundation a lot more transparent to agencies and makes us a lot less intimidating to grantseekers. It also saves us a lot of time, as we can answer many of their questions right there, at the meeting."

D. Seek feedback (including anonymous feedback) on foundation performance from current and former grantees and denied applicants.

What's the best way to improve your grants process and management? Ask the people who know—your grantees and grant applicants.

Foundations commonly evaluate the work of grantees without ever asking them to return the favor. By asking nonprofits what they think about your foundation, you show them that you respect their opinion. What's more, they usually give good feedback. Their suggestions can improve your grantmaking and your image in the community. It can also establish an important line of communication—one you can continue.

There are many creative ways to learn from your grantees, improve your practices and strive for a better grantee/grantor relationship. Here are some ideas:

- Conduct a survey, focus group and/or informal interviews with grantees and colleagues.

- Develop a feedback program where grantees and applicants can make both positive and negative comments.

- Bring in an outside evaluator, such as a representative from the larger nonprofit sector, who will look at the foundation's internal processes and conduct confidential interviews with foundation staff and board members, as well as applicants and grantees.

Peer Practices

Tips on Surveying Grantees

In 2002, the Fleishhacker Foundation and the Pottruck Family Foundation decided to jointly conduct a grantee survey. They sent a written questionnaire to 70 nonprofits through direct mail and held a focus group with respondents. Christine Elbel, executive director of the Fleishhacker Foundation, said the costs were postage and copying ($150), plus focus group food ($30). A college intern conducted most of the administrative work for the project, sending out and tabulating surveys in exchange for work-study credit.

"The Fleishhacker Foundation shifted some of its efforts based on survey feedback. We're making website updates more of a priority, and we're being more honest when people ask if we'll fund them or not," said Elbel.

"We learned that it's important to open your work to critique from the field and that the exercise gives new insight into your grantmaking practice—particularly if you work alone," said Elbel. "Otherwise, you can become too removed from current issues or stale in how you think and operate."

Elbel offered several pieces of advice for family foundations who wish to survey grantees. "Once you tabulate your results, inform your board of both the larger issues and the nuances of the project," she said. "Make sure survey responses are anonymous and keep the survey simple. Consider doing it online for added anonymity and ease of use. Don't ask for information you're not ready to consider because it may heighten expectations, such as changing your program areas or grantmaking methods."

"Not only did our self-assessment teach us how we can do better, but it also sent a message to the grantseeking public that we care what they think."

—Carrie Avery, president, Durfee Foundation

If you are going the survey route, it helps to keep all responses anonymous. This will often elicit frank and open responses. You can design your own questions, based on the kinds of information that would serve you and your grantees best. For example, you might ask current grantees:

- How would you describe your encounter with the foundation?

- What advice would you give about the future of the program?

- Is there anything the foundation could have done to better support you?

- What comments do you have on the application process itself—including the application, site visit, interview (i.e., was it difficult, manageable, helpful, hurtful, and why)?

In addition to surveying grantees, many foundations learn a lot from those grantseekers they've declined. You might ask declined grant applicants:

- How did you hear about the program?

- What factors influenced your decision to apply?

- What was the impact (on you, your staff and/or board) of your not being selected for the award?

- Would you consider reapplying to the program? Why or why not?

Once you conduct the survey, share the results as broadly as possible with your board and staff and in grantmaker forums and publications. For example, you might post results on your website, or in foundation newsletters (such as the Council's *Family Matters* or *Family Matters Now*).

Finally, tell grantees the results of the survey and the changes you plan to make based on their responses. Your answers will demonstrate your accountability, and your grantees will appreciate it.

For sample grantee surveys, see the end of this chapter.

Some excerpts of the above taken from "The Importance of Asking," by Carrie Avery, president, The Durfee Foundation, Family Matters, Summer 2001. Visit www.cof.org.

In Their Own Words

Asking for Applicant Feedback

"At the Durfee Foundation, we evaluate our grantmaking practices with the help of the community we serve. Self-assessment with our grantees was easy; we also needed to hear from the applicants who did not get grants. We had learned from the Walter and Elise Haas Fund that some of the most important feedback they received came from unsuccessful applicants. In a similar assessment, we mailed anonymous surveys to all who had applied to the program in its four-year existence. In reviewing the overwhelmingly thoughtful responses to the survey, we learned that the program is well regarded in the community—even by those who did not receive grants. The surveys helped us streamline our application forms and clarify our guidelines."

—Carrie Avery, president, Durfee Foundation

E. Respond to and act promptly on complaints.

You may not expect them, but sometimes complaints do happen. What do you do if your foundation receives a complaint from one of your grantees?

The best advice is to respond quickly. People make mistakes, and foundation board members and staff are no exception. If your foundation made an error, or there was some misunderstanding, admit the mistake and be willing to apologize. Listen to what grantees have to say and ask them how you can do better in the future. Thank them for their feedback and give them the appropriate information they need.

One foundation found the best way to receive complaints is to ask grantees for their help in fixing the problem. "One of our grantees told us that our grant agreement was confusing—that there were parts to it they didn't understand," said Jodi Allison Jennings of the Fitzpatrick Foundation. "We reviewed the agreement with them and asked them to help us rewrite it—which they did. Now it's easier for everyone to understand."

Peer Practices

Listening to Grantees

The Russell Family Foundation participated in a grantee survey through the Center for Effective Philanthropy. This really helped inform the staff on how the foundation was doing. According to Chief Executive Officer Richard Woo, "We sat down with the detailed evaluation and identified where we were performing well and where we needed to improve."

The foundation is now making changes based on the responses they received from grantees. For example, grantees who participated in the survey indicated that midyear reports were too cumbersome, especially for some of the smaller grant recipients. "Based on those responses, we decided to eliminate midyear reports for grants below $10,000 and assess those grants through our own relationships with grantees."

In sum, ask yourself:

- Would I be able to fill out my foundation's grant application quickly and easily?

- Will we use all the information that we request from grantseekers and grantees?

- How quickly do we respond to grantseeker inquiries and submissions?

- For each grant awarded, do we share the same expectations as our grantee about what the grant should achieve?

- Does our board recognize the power and responsibility we hold as funders?

- What do grantees and other nonprofits think about my foundation's grants management process?

Resources

"Assessing our Work: Evaluating Foundation Performance and Practice," *Family Matters*, Summer 2001. Visit www.cof.org.

The Family Advisor:

- *Grantmaking Issues*

- *Grant Evaluation*

- *Site Visit Companion*

Visit www.cof.org.

Grantmaking Basics: A Field Guide for Funders. Council on Foundations, 1999. Visit www.cof.org/publications.

Websites

Grantmakers for Effective Organizations—www.geofunders.org

Sample Grant Guidelines

Courtesy of the Evelyn and Walter Haas, Jr. Fund

First-time or nonrecurring applicants should submit a two- to three-page letter of inquiry. Current grantees seeking renewal funding should contact the person at the Fund with whom they have been working before submitting a new proposal or inquiry. An applicant who knows a Trustee should indicate the association in the inquiry letter, and staff will bring the application to the attention of the Trustees.

Letters of inquiry should include:

- A brief statement of the organization's purpose and goals.
- If applicable, a description of the project, the need and the target population it addresses.
- Information about the capability of the leadership to implement the proposed project.
- Short- and long-term outcomes anticipated and plans for assessing achievements.
- Grant amount needed.
- A statement about the total agency budget and the project budget, if different.
- A statement about other funding sources for the agency and/or project, specifying both committed and projected sources of support.

The Review Process

Staff will review your letter of inquiry within one month of receiving it to determine if the proposed effort fits within the Fund's giving program. If so, you will receive a call or letter from a staff member requesting additional information or a full proposal. If you are asked to submit a full proposal, we will provide an outline of questions frequently asked when reviewing a request.

During the review process, staff may research your request through telephone inquiries, meetings or site visits. They may speak with your colleagues, board members or outside experts. If staff decides to submit your request to the Trustees, they will prepare a written report and recommendations. In general, applicants can expect a decision within four months of the date their full proposal is received. This may vary, however, depending upon the dates of the trustee meetings and the number of pro-posals being considered.

Eligibility Requirements

The Fund supports organizations that are tax exempt under Section 501(c)(3) of the Internal Revenue Service Code and are not classified as private foundations under Section 509(a) of the Code. In selected cases, it may consider support for projects sponsored by governmental entities. Organizations also may submit applications through a sponsoring organization, if the sponsor has 501(c)(3) status, is not a private foundation under 509(a), and provides written authorization confirming its willingness to act as a fiscal sponsor.

The Fund will not support organizations that discriminate in their leadership, staffing, service provi-sion or on the basis of age, gender, race, ethnicity, sexual orientation, disability, national origin, politi-cal affiliation or religious belief. The Fund does, however, support selected organizations working within its guideline areas whose services target specific groups that have been subject to economic, social, political or other forms of discrimination.

Sample Acknowledgment Postcard

Courtesy of the Association of Small Foundations, www.smallfoundations.org

Dear _____,

We received your proposal request of (date) for funding of (amount) for (project description). The full proposal packet contains all appropriate materials for our review.

Your request will be presented to the foundation board at their grant review meeting, currently scheduled to take place in (month, year). We will contact you with their decision no later than (month, year).

We will contact you before then if there are further questions we may have regarding your proposal.

Sincerely,

(Name)

(Title)

Sample Grant Agreement Letter

Courtesy of The Dean and Margaret Lesher Foundation

[Date]

[Name]

[Organization]

[Address]

[City, State, Zip]

Dear [Name]:

The **Dean and Margaret Lesher Foundation** is pleased to advise you that the Board of Directors has approved a grant in the amount of $[   ] for the [Organization], in support of your [name of program] for [purpose of project]. This grant is being made in response to your proposal dated [fill in date received].

All grant awards by the **Dean and Margaret Lesher Foundation** are subject to the following conditions, in accordance with laws applicable to the Foundation, and with the policies and priorities established by the Foundation. **Funding must be limited to programs and/or services within Contra Costa County**. Any special instructions applying to this grant are also listed.

Sample Grant Agreement

Courtesy of The Dean and Margaret Lesher Foundation

PURPOSE: The grant shall be used solely for the purpose stated in the grant proposal, and shall be so designated on your organization's records. No part of the funds shall be used for any purpose other than charitable or educational.

BUDGET AND FINANCE: If this grant has been based upon a specific expense budget, a copy of that budget has been attached to this agreement. No changes may be made in the budgetary allocations of the grant award without the Foundation's written approval. Any portion of the grant not expended as set forth in the budget included in the grant proposal will be returned to the Foundation at the completion of the project or end of the grant period unless a written request is received and approved by the Foundation Board of Directors.

PAYMENT: Funds are to be paid on a date mutually agreeable to the [Name of Organization] and the **Dean and Margaret Lesher Foundation**. Please write or call the Foundation office at your earliest convenience to establish an appropriate schedule of payment.

Payment of funds is subject to any special conditions as noted below. Prior to any funds being distributed, the Foundation must have on file a countersigned copy of this grant agreement letter.

PROGRAM MONITORING, EVALUATION AND REVIEW: At the conclusion of the project or grant period, your organization is to furnish a written report within 30 days on the use of the grant to the Executive Director of the Foundation. This report should include a description and appraisal of the project or program funded under this grant. The financial portion of this report should correspond in format to the attached budget, if any, and should show a comparison of actual to budgeted expenditures.

The Foundation may monitor and conduct an evaluation of operations under this grant. Such evaluation may include a site visit from Foundation staff and/or Board to observe your program, and to discuss the program with your personnel. This evaluation may also include a review of financial and other records related to activities funded by this grant. Your organization, therefore, agrees to make such records available to authorized representatives of the Foundation.

PUBLICITY AND ACKNOWLEDGMENT: Your organization may issue a news release concerning the grant. However, the Foundation shall review the text of any release, which should be submitted to the Executive Director of the Foundation not less than ten days prior to the release date.

Other forms of acknowledgment, such as listings in program and annual reports, do not need Foundation approval.

SPECIAL CONDITIONS: The grant period is [fill in your dates]. If necessary, the end date may be adjusted with the approval of the Foundation.

In the unlikely event that your organization should fail to abide by the terms set forth in this letter of agreement, the **Dean and Margaret Lesher Foundation** may terminate the grant, upon written notice to your organization. Your organization would then be required to return to the Foundation any portion of the grant funds, including interest earned, spent for purposes not specified in this letter or not otherwise approved by the Foundation.

Continued on page 134

To confirm your understanding of and agreement to the above conditions of this grant, please have the attached copy (retain original for your file) of this letter signed by an authorized officer of your organization's Board of Directors.

By countersigning this letter, you also agree that:

(1) Your organization's charitable tax exempt status under the Internal Revenue Service has not been revoked or modified, and that if it is revoked or modified, you agree to notify the Foundation immediately.

(2) The Foundation assumes no obligation to provide other or additional support.

(3) Your organization will submit to the Executive Director of the Foundation a copy of minutes from a meeting of your Board of Directors documenting its review of the grant award and its acceptance of the terms and conditions.

Should you have any questions about the grant or the conditions set forth, please call me at (XXX) XXX-XXXX. On behalf of the **Dean and Margaret Lesher Foundation,** I extend every good wish for the success of the [name of program or project].

Sincerely,

Kathleen Odne
Executive Director

(Print or type name and position of <u>Board Officer</u> signing)

BY:

DATE:

Sample Site Visit Form

Courtesy of the Perrin Family Foundation

Site name:

Address:

Date of Visit: **Visit conducted by:**

Met with:

Purpose of Site Visit:

Amount Requested: **Program Name:**

Physical Plant:

Is infrastructure in place to accomplish what they propose in request?

Director:

_____ Is leadership an effective communicator of ideas?

_____ Does he/she relate well to people?

_____ Does the person reflect a proprietary interest or is this just a job?

_____ How long has the person been in the present position?

_____ What is their previous experience?

_____ If recent change in management, what was the cause?

Comments:

Staff:

_____ Is organization adequately staffed?

_____ Is staff motivated and engaged in their work?

Comments:

Program: Summary of specific project goals

_____ Can they be specific about what they propose to do?

_____ Is their approach feasible?

_____ Innovative?

_____ Cost effective?

Define Collaborations:

Continued on page 136

Accomplishments:

Challenges:

Evaluation methods:

Budget: Funding challenges, any specific questions about the program budget

_____ Is there a dependence on a few major donors to sustain the organization?

Comments:

Strategic Plan:

_____ Does the organization have a strategic plan? When was it made?

Describe any changes in direction for the agency:_____

Board:

Describe involvement, financial contribution; length of service:

Reminder: Be sure to…

- Ask for questions
- Explain the review and approval process
- Confirm the next steps (What they need to do, what you need to do)
- Establish a timeline for review and decisions (within a month)

Items of Concern: To be addressed at mid grant conversation.

Recommended _____   Not Recommended _____

Historical Grants:

Sample Grant Report

Courtesy of the Association of Small Foundations, www.smallfoundations.org

Cover Sheet

Name of organization:

Address:

Report prepared by (name and title):

Phone number:

Purpose of grant (see Proposal Cover Sheet):

Period covered by this report (mo/day/yr to mo/day/yr):

Please complete this Grantee Report Cover Sheet and send it back to us with responses to the enclosed set of Evaluation Questions. We request that you respond to each question in order and, if a question is not applicable to your project or organization, that you specify "NA" (for "not applicable") by the number of that question. Use as much space as you need to answer each question, while being as concise as possible.

Return this form and the Evaluation Questions to:

(Foundation name and address)

Due date:

Evaluation Questions

The following information is needed by (Foundation name) to help us monitor the activities and outcomes of your grant. If any component is not appropriate to your project, the component should be listed and followed by the letters N/A.

The Project

1. Please refer to the proposal funded by (Foundation name) and list your objectives for the proposal period. Describe the progress toward accomplishing your objectives and note the number of persons affected by your activities (when appropriate).

2. Was it necessary to make any changes in the proposed project? Is the project on schedule? Have there been any staff changes? Please explain any modifications to the proposal.

3. Briefly summarize the evaluation process for the project. What did you learn from your own evaluation?

4. What do you consider your most notable project accomplishments during the past year?

5. What were the greatest challenges/obstacles you faced while developing and implementing this project?

6. Describe any lessons you learned in carrying out the project objectives (lessons dealing with process, strategies, unexpected problems or outcomes, etc.).

Continued on page 138

7. What other organizations/coalitions have you worked with in initiating and implementing this project?

8. With respect to the work supported by this grant, what problems and prospects do you foresee for the future?

Financial Information

9. Please provide total project income and expense information to date. Describe any budget changes or other financial adaptations required by any unforeseen situation(s).

10. Submit a copy of your most recently completed monthly financial statemen (which should include year-to-date information) and, if you have completed a fiscal year in the last six months, send your audited financial statement.

11. Indicate how this project will be funded in the future.

General

12. Attach copies of any significant materials, newsletters, brochures, articles, etc. which shed light on the project's or your organization's activities.

Sample Grantee Survey

Courtesy of the Fleishhacker Foundation

The Fleishhacker Foundation's Grantseeker Survey

Thank you for agreeing to participate in this survey designed to collect information on, and develop an understanding of, the challenges grantseekers face when applying for financial support from foundations.

Please circle your answers where appropriate; with open-ended questions, please feel free to use additional paper if necessary. Please be as candid as possible and return this survey to the Fleishhacker Foundation. Thank you!

1. What is your current title?

    a. Executive Director

    b. Development Director

    c. Program Director

    d. Other (please specify);_____

2. How many years have you worked in the nonprofit sector?

    a. 0-2 years

    b. 3-5 years

    c. 6-10 years

    d. 10+ years

3. What is your organization's budget?

    a. less than $100,000

    b. $100,001 - $500,000

    c. $500,001 - $1,000,000

    d. $1,000,001 - $5,000,000

    e. greater than $5,000,000

4. To the best of your knowledge, what percentage of your organization's funding comes from the following sources?

    Small foundations (3 or fewer staff members)? _____%

    Large foundations (more than 3 staff members)? _____%

Continued on page 140

5. What percentage of your organization's funding comes from San Francisco Bay Area-based foundations?: _____%

    Please circle the level of agreement to the following statements:

    1 Strongly Agree

    2 Somewhat Agree

    3 Neutral

    4 Disagree

    5 Strongly Disagree

6. I have a good relationship with funders. 1 2 3 4 5

7. Most foundations/foundation staff respect their grantees. 1 2 3 4 5

8. I consider funders to be partners in my work. 1 2 3 4 5

9. The grant seeking process is frustrating. 1 2 3 4 5

10. Site visits are an effective way for grantmakers to learn about our organization. 1 2 3 4 5

11. Most foundations/staff I work with make site visits. 1 2 3 4 5

12. Most foundations offer clear guidelines and explain their funding priorities clearly. 1 2 3 4 5

13. Most foundations explain the grant review process and timetable in a way that makes sense. 1 2 3 4 5

14. Most foundations/foundation staff I work with return phone calls in a timely manner. 1 2 3 4 5

15. Most foundations/foundation staff I work with communicate about the status of pending proposals. 1 2 3 4 5

16. Most foundations/staff I work with make an effort to understand our proposals. 1 2 3 4 5

17. Most foundations/staff I work with make an effort to understand our organization. 1 2 3 4 5

18. Most foundations/staff I work with are knowledgeable about the issues and/or challenges that our organization faces. 1 2 3 4 5

19. Most foundations/staff I work with provide advice that is generally sound. 1 2 3 4 5

20. Most foundations/staff I work with make reasonable requests for additional information when reviewing a proposal. 1 2 3 4 5

21. Most foundations/staff I work with are honest in their dealings with grantees. 1 2 3 4 5

22. Most foundations/staff I work with seem truly engaged in, and committed to, their work. 1 2 3 4 5

23. Most foundations/staff I work with have reasonable application/proposal requirements. 1 2 3 4 5

24. Most foundations/staff I work with have reasonable reporting requirements. 1 2 3 4 5

Open-ended questions (please use additional paper if necessary)

25. What are the best aspects of the process of securing funding from foundations?

26. What are the most frustrating aspects of dealing with foundations?

27. If you could change one thing about the process of applying for a grant (or working with foundations), what would it be?

28. What improvements would you suggest in these areas?
    a. Grant application/proposal requirements (written document)
    b. Communication with foundation/founda
    c. Site Visits
    d. Reporting requirements
    e. Other:

29. Have e-mail and web sites improved communication with foundations and/or facilitated getting information about funding priorities? If not, why not?

30. If you had one piece of advice for foundation staff as to how to do their jobs better, what would it be?

CHAPTER 7
Strive for Accessibility and Transparency

PRINCIPLE VII:

WE WELCOME PUBLIC INTEREST AND COMMUNICATE OPENLY.

Good communication drives good grantmaking. There should be no question about *whether* you communicate. After all, you communicate every day, in everything you do. It's *how* you communicate that matters.

Too often, family foundations think they should keep quiet about what they do. Perhaps they feel overworked and understaffed and don't want to "put the word out" for fear they will be deluged by a storm of inquiries and proposals. Others may feel uncomfortable publicizing the foundation's good work, concerned it might come across as bragging. Or they might simply prefer to give in private.

All of these are legitimate concerns. Yet, there are ways to communicate about your foundation and its grantees, and still honor the family's desire for privacy. For example, as part of your communications, you can list your preferred contact method.

Most foundations find that communicating proactively actually helps them fulfill their mission. Instead of receiving many more proposals unrelated to their mission, they get more proposals that match their mission—actually saving them time in the end. And by communicating openly and welcoming interest, they build the public's trust.

In the past, this trust has been a little shaky. Following an era of corporate scandals, Congress has put the nonprofit sector under inquiry. Foundations—particularly private foundations—are receiving great scrutiny from lawmakers and the media. In 2004, the Senate Finance Committee sparked a lot of attention on Capitol Hill and elsewhere by proposing reforms for the nonprofit sector which, if enacted, could change the way foundations operate and meet their missions.

Perhaps public policy has remained outside of your foundation's normal business scope. In the current legislative climate, however, it may be time for a change in approach to develop relationships with your elected officials. In the absence of correct information, it is easy for misinformation to get widely communicated.

> ### IN THIS CHAPTER
>
> - How to craft clear, grantee-friendly guidelines and procedures
> - How to conduct respectful site visits
> - Tips for improving grantee/grantor relations
> - Ways to solicit feedback from grantees and grantseekers
> - How to respond to complaints

"If we don't tell our story, someone else will. What is the chance they will get it right?"

—Carol Stabler, director of communications, The Meadows Foundation

Communications will help you in every aspect of your work—but it's bigger than that. When you communicate about the good work you do, you give the public an opportunity to understand what family foundations are about. By welcoming interest and communicating openly, you help educate the media, lawmakers and the public. In doing so, you help the entire charitable field.

Here's a summary of what communications can do:

- Demonstrate to the public what has been done with funds used.
- Better inform grantseekers on what your foundation will—and will not—fund, preventing them from wasting time by not preparing ineligible proposals.
- Raise the visibility of your grantees' work.
- Attract other potential funding collaborators.
- Show lawmakers that foundations are accountable and transparent, thereby relieving the pressure for government regulation.

This section will show you just how easy communications can be—and how much better it is when you're no longer the best kept secret in town.

Practice Options for Principle VII

A. Make public (online and in print) the foundation's board of directors, mission, guidelines, grant process (including whether unsolicited proposals are accepted), finances, procedures, timetable, grantee list with amounts and purpose, etc.

Start by doing your research.

Make a list of all the audiences you want to reach. Think about your internal audience—the board and staff, for example—and also your external audiences—grantees, grant applicants, your foundation colleagues, your community, the press and so forth.

Ask yourselves: *How are we currently communicating with our audiences? How do they perceive our foundation? What works and what doesn't work?*

You might ask a few different audience groups (grantees or grant applicants, for example) for their feedback and ideas. Ask them, either in person or through an anonymous survey: *What are we doing well? How clear are our grant guidelines, applications, website, annual reports?* This can help you understand how your message is getting across, what is working and what you might improve.

Once you gain a sense of how you currently communicate, you can apply that knowledge to new and improved communications. It starts with the basics. Your foundation should publish (either print or online) the following information:

- Annual Form 990-PF.
- Board of Directors list.
- Mission.
- Grant guidelines.
- Grant procedures and process (including whether unsolicited proposals are accepted).
- Timeline for accepting and approving grant proposals.
- Grantees list with grant purpose and amounts.
- Asset size and other financial information.

Grantseekers and the public welcome this information, which explains what your foundation does, who runs the foundation and how the grantmaking process works. It increases your foundation's accountability in a simple—and necessary—way.

Make this information readily available in your annual report, foundation newsletter and other printed materials. Of course, one of the fastest and easiest ways for you to share this information is on a website.

In Their Own Words

Publicizing Audits

"Placing our audit on the Web increased confidence in our claims to be efficient in our work. The media were amazed at our 'audaciousness' in doing it. And we were gratified with the positive response from the grantmaking and grantseeking community. By opening up all of our books, procedures, selection processes, history and administrative costs, we are becoming a more user-friendly organization and hold ourselves to the same standards we apply to our grantseekers."

—*Al Castle, executive director, Samuel N. & Mary Castle Foundation*

Communicating on the Web

The Web is often the first place people look when seeking information. Websites express a family foundation's mission and communicate its value to trustees, nonprofits and the community. If you don't already have one, your family foundation should consider a website.

Websites have a practical side as well: They save everyone time. Instead of spending valuable minutes on the phone, you might simply point people to your site. According to Jodi Allison Jennings, program associate of the Fitzpatrick Foundation in San Francisco, "I direct callers right to our website. This saves me time from walking them through all the information they need—because it's all there!"

Websites help you:

- Improve your transparency
- Communicate with board members or staff
- Share program information and guidelines with grant seekers and the public
- Streamline the grants cycle through online applications, eligibility screening, proposal review and grantee reporting.

When creating a website, aim for one that enables your audience to access information in an easy and efficient way. Your site should provide background information about your foundation, its board, grant guidelines and process, news, resources and more. Some foundations even include downloadable applications, grant report forms and the foundation's annual report on their site.

Many foundations fear that going online will inundate them with applications. However, they quickly find that the *more* information they publish, the more targeted proposals they receive.

For example, one family foundation recently posted its grant guidelines and contact information on the Internet. Members sat back and waited, wondering if hundreds of applications would come pouring in the next day. They didn't.

The staff experienced only a minimal increase in the number of inquiries they received. What changed was that most of the new inquiries came in via e-mail—which made responding quick and easy. As a

---

Public Disclosure—What the Law Says

As a private foundation, you are obligated to make the following documents available to the public:

- Form 990-PF, the annual information return filed with the IRS, for the three most recent years
- Form 1023, the application for federal tax-exempt status (and all related correspondence with the IRS), if the foundation had a copy of the application on July 15, 1987 or filed its application after that date.

Your foundation must furnish a copy of these documents to anyone who requests them in person (on the same day) or in writing (within 30 days). Foundations must also provide copies of these returns and exemption applications for inspection at their principal office (or at an alternative location, if the foundation has no office) during normal business hours.

As an alternative, your foundation may make these documents "widely available" to the public—for example, by posting them on your website. GuideStar (www.guidestar.org), a 501(c)(3) public charity, posts all 990s, obtained from the IRS, on its website. However, because GuideStar doesn't include some attachments, this may or may not satisfy the public disclosure requirements.

result of this new communications medium, the foundation identified a few new grantees whom they wouldn't have found otherwise.

For information about the Foundation Center's Web service for foundations (called Foundation Folders), visit www.fdncenter.org or contact 212/807-2481.

B. IDENTIFY AND MAKE PUBLIC A POINT OF CONTACT FOR THE FOUNDATION.

Who's your point of contact?

It helps to designate one person as the main point of contact for your foundation. This will likely be a staff person, the board chair or another board member.

People like talking to people—not organizations. Think about how you feel when calling an organization for the first time. If you have a name in advance, it likely puts you more at ease and makes you feel a little more connected.

Without a point of contact, your foundation could seem like a nameless, faceless organization—and one that seems less approachable.

Here's another tip: Ask your foundation's point of contact to record caller-friendly outgoing phone messages. This will give callers the information they need and reduce the number of calls they have to return. Here are some phone message suggestions, some more obvious than others:

- Clearly state the foundation's name and the point of contact's name.
- Let callers know when they are likely to reach someone in the office, especially if you are only staffed part time or don't have any staff.
- Direct callers to your website for answers to frequently asked questions.
- If you don't have a website, list a brief and clear description of your giving program and limitations.
- Inform callers of the next deadline for grant proposal submissions and the approximate date of grant decisions.
- Ask callers to leave their name, mailing address or e-mail address to receive your latest annual report and a copy of your grant guidelines.
- Thank them for calling.

Make sure that anyone answering the phone can respond to any of these inquiries, including the status of a pending proposal. This will not only help grantseekers, but also minimize the administrative work on your end.

In Their Own Words

Doing Well on the Web

"Our communities are the customers we seek to serve, and we believe we should be as transparent as possible. We know our website is working from what our grantees tell us. In a recent grantee survey, grantees said the web is our most helpful communications tool; it's where they get the most usable information. We include a grant application and budget template, as well as a midpoint and year-end report form that grantees may download. We also have a searchable database of all our environmental grantees and their projects."

—Richard Woo, chief executive officer, The Russell Family Foundation

"We have a rule: We return every phone call as soon as possible."

—Jane Stamstad, executive director, James R. Thorpe Foundation

C. RESPOND TO REQUESTS FOR INFORMATION PROMPTLY AND IN NO MORE THAN 30 DAYS.

It sounds like a lesson in Etiquette 101, but don't shrug it off. Everyone appreciates a prompt response. When you don't respond to requests in a timely way, your foundation appears less credible—or worse, unapproachable.

You want your foundation to appear open and accessible to the public. If you can't get back to someone right away, be honest. Give them a quick e-mail or a call to let them know that you are tied up at the moment and will respond as quickly as you can. You'll find people are much more forgiving if they hear *some* response instead of *no* response.

That said, we're all human, and sometimes we make mistakes. What if you find a sticky note, weeks later, with a message you never returned? Call the person back immediately and admit your mistake. Apologize and ask them what information you can provide for them today.

This guideline applies whether or not you are interested in a proposal. If someone has taken the time and made the effort to send in an inquiry or proposal, they deserve the courtesy of a response, even if the response is "no thanks."

D. Prepare and distribute (online or in print) an annual report (or letter for small foundations).

An annual report is your foundation's report to the community—a summary of the activities for the prior year and a record of grants and issues funded. Often, the annual report serves as a foundation's most important communications tool. For smaller foundations, it may be the only publication your foundation produces.

According to a recent Council on Foundations survey, only one in 20 family foundations produce an annual report. Some said they didn't have the time or resources to create one. Those foundations should know this: Annual reports don't need to be fancy and expensive in order to be *effective*.

Annual reports may be a simple, typed document listing the previous year's donors and grants. They can take the form of a one-pager, a newsletter, a brochure, a booklet or a posting on your website. Plus, the costs you incur for producing an annual report qualify as part of your minimum distribution (payout) for that year.

One family foundation found a simple and inexpensive way to write its annual report. Each holiday season, the Albert J. Speh, Jr. & Claire R. Speh Foundation mails a letter (similar to a family newsletter) that updates others on foundation news in the year past year. The letter talks about its board and what the foundation sees as a result of its grantmaking. The board said it takes only a short time to write the letter, and they print it on holiday stationery (thereby saving costs for printer and design fees). The mailing costs approximately $200 each year.

If you're just getting started on your annual report—or looking to update it—consider including some of the following information:

- Year, name and geographic focus of the foundation.
- Address, telephone number and website address.
- Mission, vision, values, brief history and purpose of the foundation.
- Statement by the board chair and/or the executive director highlighting some aspect of the foundation or discussing the importance of philanthropy.
- Overview of the organization and governing structure, identifying members of the board, officers and staff.
- Statement of grant activity during the year, identifying the program category, recipient and amount of each grant.
- Narrative description of several key grants.
- Section outlining the grant program and policies and detailing the application procedures

Peer Practices

Annual Reports Set Expectations

One thing that has helped the Self Family Foundation serve the community is their constant and clear communication with the public. The foundation's annual report describes very clearly the types of programs and initiatives they will fund and the funding process. Relationships that the trustees and staff have with the community also help them to understand its needs and tap into assets lying dormant. According to President Frank Wideman, "I think we have a responsibility to clearly communicate our mission to the public so they'll know exactly what kind of assistance to expect from us and what kinds of changes we're working to effect."

- Description of special programs or initiatives undertaken.

- List of the financial institutions holding the foundation's funds.

- Report of the independent public accountant who audits the books, accompanied by financial statements.

Once your annual report is ready, you should distribute it widely—to your extended family, grantees, potential grantseekers and the larger community. Take your reports to meetings, conferences and other events. Mail your report to board members, grantees, reporters, elected officials, foundation colleagues and others. Some foundations even publish their annual reports online—either on their own website or through an outside service such as The Foundation Center (www.fdncenter.org).

To save on printing costs, the Dyson Foundation posts its report on its website and then mails postcards to key contacts announcing that the latest report is available online.

Quick Tip

Creating an Annual Report

- **Start a folder** at the beginning of the year. Use it to save lists of grants, speeches by board members and staff, newspaper clips, news releases, fund reports, photos, etc.

- **Borrow ideas** from the annual reports of similar-sized foundations. Look for other foundation annual reports at Council on Foundations conferences or through the Council's Wilmer Shields Rich Awards, www.cof.org.

- **Write as you go** about grants and events, when the details are fresh.

- **Ask grantees** for photographs, and take advantage of events that occur throughout the year by hiring a photographer or taking photos yourself.

- **Consider the tone** you want to use. Most foundations strive to be regarded as down-to-earth and accessible.

E. Train the board and staff on how to respond to the media, legislators and other audiences.

Media and lawmakers occasionally contact foundations to learn more about their mission or the field in general. Your board and staff should learn how to handle inquiries, so *you* can frame your foundation's story in your own words. First you will want to designate a media contact.

Choosing a Media Contact

Just as you chose one person to be your foundation's point of contact, you also need to choose one person to be the *media* contact. This may be different from your general point of contact. In smaller foundations, the main media contact is usually the board chair or executive director. However, if one of your board members has experience working with the media or in public policy, you might choose that person instead. For larger foundations, the media contact is usually the executive director or a communications officer.

Once you choose a primary media contact for your foundation, all media inquiries should be directed to this person—and *only* this person. It is vital that there be one voice for the foundation, giving the foundation more control over the message it sends out.

Make sure that your media contact is fully trained in how to work with reporters, legislators and other audiences. You might want to ask someone in your community (for example, a colleague skilled in public relations) to provide you with some good ideas.

Here are a few tips for working with reporters and other audiences:

DO:

- Write down two or three points you want to make and use them early in the exchange.
- When appropriate, relate your responses to your two or three key points.
- Tell the truth.
- Watch your body language and maintain eye contact.
- If you cannot answer a question, promise to get back to them as soon as possible; ask when their deadline is and meet it.
- Keep your answers brief and focused.
- Speak in clear, everyday language and take time in answering questions.
- Remain calm, even if hostile questions are asked.

DON'T:

- Speculate; just stick to the facts.
- Become defensive or argumentative or say "no comment."
- Become emotional.
- Say anything "off the record." There is no such thing.

For more information, read the Grantmaker's Communication Manual, *Council on Foundations and Forum of RAGS, 1998. Visit* www.cof.org.

Sending the Right Message

In addition to training a media contact, your entire board and staff should understand the function of communications, both internally and externally. Sometimes, they may not be clear on what message the foundation should be sending. Here are some ideas to encourage them to get the word out—and to get it out right.

- Ask yourselves why your foundation exists. Develop a simple answer of under 10 words that members can recite when asked. Print this on your business card or other materials.

- Give board, staff and volunteers an index card listing the basic facts about the foundation (vision, mission, contact information, etc) and its grantmaking program (focus areas, limitations, submission deadlines).

- Remind your colleagues to describe grants in terms of human problems solved—and encourage them to share these stories with others

- Provide them with the tools for writing, public speaking, using the Web and more.

The better trained your board members and staff are on communicating, the more accurate will be information they send to the public. Look for communications training at Council on Foundations conferences, or other offerings by the Council or your regional association of grantmakers. If there are no local communications courses available, try videotaping staff and board members responding candidly to common questions concerning the foundation.

In Their Own Words

A Foundation with One Voice

"The staff follows a media protocol as established and approved by the president. Whenever the media calls, the call is directed to the communications desk, where needs and deadlines are assessed. The director of communications meets with the president or her designee to develop the appropriate response. By following this protocol, we make sure that responses are timely and thorough and that the values of the foundation are reflected in all communication with members of the press."

—Linda P. Evans, president and CEO, The Meadows Foundation

F. DEVELOP A STRATEGY FOR REACHING OUT TO THE MEDIA, LEGISLATORS AND OTHER AUDIENCES.

Your foundation should develop a strategy for reaching out to the media, legislators and other target audiences. The more you build relationships with these audiences, the more you educate them on the important role of foundations—thereby helping the field, as a whole, improving its transparency and building a positive image.

Here are some ideas you might include in your strategy:

- **Develop a targeted media list**. Identify media and reporters who are important to your foundation and grantees. Look for opportunities to meet with them individually and develop a relationship so they'll know you and call you when they are writing stories.

- **Develop an information kit for the media and federal and state legislators**. Create an information kit containing a fact sheet on your foundation, your latest news release, examples of successful grant programs, a chart showing how foundation dollars are spent (i.e., grants, administrative expenses) and brief biographies of foundation spokespeople. *(See sample at the end of this chapter.)*

- **Pursue regular media outreach opportunities**. Pitch news stories when you have news. Work with grantees to organize "grant results" ceremonies; invite elected officials and the press to attend.

- **Organize a small group of grantmakers** to meet with your elected officials. Ideally, the group should be composed of representatives from a variety of grantmaking organizations. Prepare an agenda and talking points in advance *(See www.foundationsonthehill.org for more information and samples.)* Talk about your foundation's work, the importance of philanthropy and the charitable sector, and/or a specific piece of legislation that concerns your foundations. *See the sidebar "Can You Lobby?"*

- **Talk to your community**. Make a speech at a local business organization highlighting how your foundation makes a difference in the community. Develop, or encourage grantees to develop, an op-ed column for the local newspaper, a feature highlighting foundation goals and outcomes in relation to a local "hot" issue (e.g., education, environment, the economy).

- **Encourage grantees to share results and outcomes with the media**. Provide grantees with a few foundation information kits and sample news releases to announce their grants. Support your grantees' media outreach.

This sounds like a lot—and it is. Your foundation doesn't have to take all of these steps at once. Examine what you want to accomplish and perhaps choose one or two ideas to focus on per year.

It is critical that communications be part of your foundation's overall strategic plan—and that all grantmaking initiatives, policy changes and so forth be developed in concert with your communications strategy.

Can You Lobby?

As a private foundation, you can contact your member of Congress about charitable reform legislation.

Although in general private foundations are prohibited by law from lobbying, they can engage in self-defense activities. In other words, you can advocate for or against specific legislation that relates directly to the powers, duties and tax exempt status of foundations and the tax-deductibility of contributions. For example, you can meet with legislators or write letters urging them to oppose increasing the payout rate. All self-defense lobbying must be direct lobbying (foundations make contact with legislators and staff); grassroots lobbying (when foundations urge others to make such contacts) is not permitted. For more information on advocacy, see chapter 3.

For more information, see Sample Ways to Engage in Public Policy at the end of this chapter, and contact the Council's Government Relations Department at government@cof.org.

In sum, ask yourself:

- What works well about our current communications strategies? What could we improve?

- How do we make publicly available information on who, what and how we fund?

- How quickly does our foundation respond to requests for information?

- Has our foundation identified someone to be a media contact?

- How prepared are we to respond to inquiries from the media, grantseekers, public officials and other audiences?

- How can we be sure everyone involved in the foundation (board and staff) speaks with the same message?

- How might grantees provide us with their suggestions on our written materials?

- How can we contribute to a positive image of philanthropy and family foundations?

Resources

"Communicating Effectively." By Martha Cooley. *Family Foundation Library Series: Management.* Council on Foundations, 1997, pp 103–112. Visit www.cof.org/publications.

Communications Handbook: A Basic Publicity Guide. Council of Michigan Foundations, 1994. www.cmif.org.

Grantmakers Communications Manual. By Christopher McNamara. Council on Foundations and Regional Association of Grantmakers, 1998. Item #305. Visit www.cof.org/publications.

The Jossey-Bass Guide to Strategic Communications for Nonprofits: A Step-by-Step Guide to Working with the Media. Jossey-Bass Publishers, 1999. www.josseybass.com.

How Foundations Garble Their Message and Lose Their Audience: Bad Words for Good. By Tony Proscio. New York: Edna McConnell Clark Foundation, 2001.

Sample Communications Worksheet

Adapted from IMPACS 1999-2000, www.civicus.org

Note: *The following sample worksheet is an example of one way to approach your communications plan. It may be much more extensive than you want or need at this time. However, you might find some of the questions and action items useful as you think through your own communications.*

Developing a Communications Plan

1. Who are we?

- Who are we?
- What is our foundation's history?
- What do we stand for? What do we do? Why do we do it?
- What is our identity?
- Who do we aim to serve?
- How effective are we in meeting our aim and objectives?
- What has changed for the better as a result of our work?

2. How are we perceived?

- What is our foundation's profile at different levels?
- Is our foundation well known?
- Are the issues we deal with commonly known about and reported on in the media or in other forums?
- How does the outside world respond to the issues we are involved in?
- How does the outside world perceive our foundation and its work?
- How is this different from how we see ourselves?
- How do we compete with, or complement, other organizations?
- How can we learn more about how people perceive us?

3. What are our goals and objectives?

- What is our foundation's vision and mission?
- What do we want to achieve and how will we achieve it?
- What indicators have we set to measure our success?

4. What do we want to achieve through our communications plan?

- Why do we need a communications plan?
- What do we want to achieve through it?
- How will this help to achieve our aims and objectives?
- How will we measure whether we have been successful?

Continued on page 156

5. Who do we want to communicate with and why?

- Who are our different target audiences/groups?
- What is our reason for communicating with each one of them?
- What do we want the people we aim to reach to know, think, feel or do as a result of our communication activity?
- How will we measure our success?

6. What are our key messages for our different target groups?

- Develop simple, clear and compelling key messages for each different group.
- Capture your key message in a sentence, even better would be in a slogan.
- Working through the previous steps will help you to arrive at your key messages.

7. What is the best way to communicate with each target group?

- Now you are ready to come up with strategies for communicating with each group that you have identified.
- Remind yourselves what you want to achieve and then ask yourselves how this will best be achieved.
- Develop your different strategies as part of your promotion plan, e.g. get more stories into mass media, revamp your newsletter.

8. Getting the plan into action

- What will it take to implement your communication plan?
- What will each strategy cost in time and resources?
- Develop mini-budgets for each strategy and then an overall budget.
- Do we have the money and resources to do it?
- Draw up a schedule/timelines.

9. Implementing our plan

- Decide how you will implement your plan.
- Write down who is responsible for what and by when, and who is responsible overall.

10. Monitoring and evaluation

- Check that all tasks get done.
- Monitor progress with plans.
- Evaluate afterwards in relation to measurable goals set out

You will then be ready to develop your next communications plan for the year or two, based on your learning from this plan.

Sample Communications Schedule

Adapted from the Vancouver Foundation

Audience: _____

Messages: _____

ACTIVITY	JAN	FEB	MAR	APR	MAY	JUN	JUL	AUG	SEP	OCT	NOV	DEC
Publications												
Newsletter												
Annual Report												
Family Mailings												
Web site												
Events												
Board meetings												
Site visits												
Grant awards												
Reports and mailings												
President's letter												
News releases												
Contact with Legislators												

Sample Press Kit

An information folder, or "press kit" as it's commonly called, can be a succinct tool to get your information out. For example, you might give one to reporters after an interview or send it to the media along with a press release. You can also use your kit as a handout when one of your foundation leaders gives a speech.

Include the following in a folder, and call it your kit:

- **Your foundation's information**
  Contact name, number, e-mail, Web address
  Mission statement
  Background/history
  President's biography
  Fun facts about the foundation

- **A fact sheet about family foundations**
  What is a family foundation?
  Statistics on giving (see the Council on Foundations or the Foundation Center)

- **Your grantees**
  Case studies with photos give a "face to philanthropy"

- **Recent press releases**
  What's your news? Make sure it's worthy of press attention.

- **Additional materials**
  A recent annual report (if not too bulky)
  Past press clips
  Relevant articles about your grantees or about family foundations

Sample Ways to Engage in Public Policy

Ten Ways for Family Foundations to Engage in Public Policy

This list highlights some of the many ways that family foundations may engage in public policy. The assistance of experienced legal counsel should always be considered to help navigate through the federal rules for engaging in policy. Family foundations may engage in:

1. Direct communications with legislators or their staff about a general issue of concern. To use this lobbying exception these direct communications may not either refer to specific legislation or legislative proposal, or if specific legislation or proposal is referenced, no view may be expressed on such legislation.

2. Direct communications with legislators or their staff is also permitted on matters that might affect the foundation's existence, powers, duties or tax-exempt status. This is often referred to as self-defense lobbying. This exception does not extend to communications with the general public.

3. Grassroots communications to the public about a policy issue if:

   ■ The communication does not contain any reference to specific legislation or legislative proposal.

   ■ The communication references specific legislation or legislative proposal but does not express a view on the legislation or proposal.

   ■ The communication references specific legislation or legislative proposal and indicates a position on the issue but does not encourage the communication's recipients to contact legislators or provide information (e.g., legislators' names or contact information) or a mechanism to facilitate such contact.

4. Communications with executive officials (i.e., president, governors, mayors) or their staff about a policy issue where the official or staff member will not participate in the formulation of legislation discussed. If the official or staff member will participate in the formulation of legislation, the communication should either not include a reference to specific legislation or legislative proposal or should not express a view on the legislation or proposal.

5. Communications with administrative bodies to influence regulations or other implementation of existing laws.

6. Participating in class action lawsuits or similar public interest litigation in attempts to influence judicial bodies.

7. Responding to written requests from a legislative body (not a single legislator) for technical assistance on pending legislation.

8. Sharing the results of nonpartisan analysis, study or research on a legislative issue.

9. Discussion of board social, economic and similar policy issues requiring legislative solution so long as the discussion does not address the merits of specific legislation.

Private lobbying activity taken by foundation managers on their own time and at their own expense is also permissible.

Sample Letters to Legislators

Courtesy of www.foundationsonthehill.org

Requesting a Meeting

(Date)

The Honorable (full name)
(Room #, Name of Building) (Room #, Name of Building)
U.S. House of Representatives/Senate
Washington, DC 20515/20510

Re: Request for Meeting

Dear Representative or Senator (last name):

On behalf of the foundation community in your district, I am writing to request the opportunity for a small group of foundation executives to meet with you. Ideally, we would like to arrange the meeting here in your home district at a time that suits your schedule.

I am executive director of the Jones Foundation, which has $25 million in assets. We make grants totaling $2 million annually, mostly in Ohio. Our most recent data indicate that there are 24 grant-making foundations in your district with combined assets of more than $120 million, making grants annually of $7.5 million.

As you know, foundations are regulated almost exclusively by the Internal Revenue Code and the resulting Treasury regulations. Consequently, your position on the Ways and Means Committee is very important to us and we are pleased you are representing us in this capacity.

From time to time, tax issues of vital importance to grantmaking foundations come before your committee. We are requesting a brief meeting to help you better understand what we are doing to help your district. (Indicate specific issues here.) Finally, we would like to share with you our concerns about certain issues we see on the horizon.

In a few days, I will call your office to confirm receipt of this letter and to speak with your appointments secretary about possible dates. Thank you in advance for your attention to our concerns.

Sincerely,

cc: _____ (name)

L.A. for Tax Issues

Meeting Confirmation

(Date)

The Honorable _____
Room #, Name of Building
U.S. House of Representatives/Senate
Washington, DC 20515/20510

Re: Meeting of (date of meeting)

Dear Representative/Senator (last name):

On behalf of the foundation community in your (state, district, area), I want to thank you for agreeing to meet with us on (date). For your information, I have attached a list of those foundation executives expected to join me in our meeting with you. While legislation affecting the grantmaking community is not necessarily an annual occurrence, we are regulated by the tax code, and tax bills do have a tendency to touch our lives very deeply from time to time.

Therefore, we feel it is most important for you to have a clear understanding of current developments with respect to foundations in your (state, district, area). To facilitate such understanding in advance of our meeting, I have enclosed three items: (1) a list of those grantees who have received the most assistance in your (state, district, area), (2) a list of the most active foundations in your (state, district, area), and (3) the annual reports of the foundations that will be represented at our meeting. I hope you will have a chance to look at this information prior to our meeting on ____; we will be happy to answer any questions you might have at that time.

In addition to discussing recent foundation activity in (state, district, area), here are a few other issues we would like to discuss if time permits: (enclose one-page descriptions of legislative issues currently before Congress that impact foundation grantmaking).

Your attention to these concerns is deeply appreciated, and we value any assessment or advice you can give us.

Sincerely,

cc: _____ (name)

L.A. for Tax Issues

Part III: Family Legacy

We have a governing board that establishes the mission, guides the operations, oversees the effectiveness and ensures the ethical conduct of the foundation. Authority is vested in the governing board as a whole, and each member is equipped to advance the foundation's mission. We consider multiple strategies to further our mission. Our governing board exercises active fiscal oversight. **We recognize and act upon our obligations to multiple stakeholders: the donor and the donor's family, grantees and grantseekers, the public and governmental bodies.** We respect our nonprofit partners' missions and expertise and strive for relationships based on candor, understanding and fairness. We welcome public interest and communicate openly. **Our governing board respects donor intent and later generations' interests while also considering the demands of a changing world.** We plan for family leadership continuity. We have a governing board that establishes the mission, guides the operations, oversees the effectiveness and ensures the ethical conduct of the foundation. Authority is vested in the governing board as a whole, and each member is equipped to advance the foundation's mission. **We consider multiple strategies to further our mission.** Our governing board exercises active fiscal oversight. We recognize and act upon our obligations to multiple stakeholders: the donor and the donor's family, grantees and grantseekers, the public and governmental bodies. **We respect our nonprofit partners' missions and expertise and strive for relationships based on candor, understanding and fairness.** We welcome public interest and communicate openly. Our governing board respects donor intent and later generations' interests while also considering the demands of a changing world. We plan for family leadership continuity. **We have a governing board that establishes the mission, guides the operations, oversees the effectiveness and ensures the ethical conduct of the foundation.** Authority is vested in the governing board as a whole, and each member is equipped to advance the foundation's mission. We consider multiple strategies to further our mission. **Our governing board exercises active fiscal oversight.** We recognize and act upon our obligations to multiple stakeholders: the donor and the donor's family, grantees and grantseekers, the public and governmental bodies. We respect our nonprofit partners' missions and expertise and strive for relationships based on candor, understanding and fairness. **We welcome public interest and communicate openly.** Our governing board respects donor intent and later generations' interests while also considering the demands of a changing world. **We plan for family leadership continuity.** We have a governing board that establishes the mission, guides the operations, oversees the effectiveness and ensures the ethical conduct of the foundation. **Authority is vested in the governing board as a whole, and each member is equipped to advance the foundation's mission.** We consider multiple strategies to further our mission. Our governing board

CHAPTER 8
Consider Your Past and Future

PRINCIPLE VIII:

OUR GOVERNING BOARD RESPECTS DONOR INTENT AND LATER GENERATIONS' INTERESTS WHILE ALSO CONSIDERING THE DEMANDS OF A CHANGING WORLD.

As family foundations evolve, most boards must perform a balancing act between three very different goals. They must:

- Honor the intent of the original donor
- Recognize the interests of later generations
- Respond to the demands of a changing world.

Seem impossible? For some foundations over many years, it might be. These goals may grow mutually exclusive—or seem contradictory. There are times when foundations must choose just one or two as their primary purpose.

Yet, there is a way for your foundation to embrace all three goals. Though you may want to see your donor intent carry on in perpetuity, communities and people change over time. If you allow your foundation to adapt to these changes, you will serve your grantees better. In addition, you will help new members of the board, who grew up in different times and perhaps in different cultures, feel more fulfilled by their work.

If it takes a charitable purpose to start a foundation, perhaps it takes flexibility to sustain it. The practice options in this chapter will help you find the right balance for your foundation.

> **IN THIS CHAPTER**
>
> - How to document and preserve your foundation's history and donor intent
> - How to balance the donor's wishes with changing needs
> - Why flexibility can keep your foundation strong
> - How to deal with family challenges and conflict.

"We want to involve the next generation now to help them prepare for the responsibilities of wealth. Our hope is that in working together on charitable giving, we can nurture generosity and foster compassionate values in the next generations."

—*Alan K. Davis, program officer, Ken R. Davis Foundation*

PRACTICE OPTIONS FOR PRINCIPLE VIII

HONORING INTENT

A. ENCOURAGE LIVING DONORS TO DOCUMENT THEIR INTENTIONS WHILE TAKING INTO ACCOUNT THE FLEXIBILITY SUCCEEDING GENERATIONS MAY NEED TO GOVERN THE FOUNDATION.

Donor intent refers to the charitable giving actions, legacy and intentions of the original donor (also called *founder*) of a foundation. Defining and drafting a statement of donor intent can be difficult. Not only must donors determine—and describe—the values they wish to impart through the foundation, but also must think about how these values will endure in the future, after they have died.

If donors don't communicate these values while they are living, board members are left with no choice but to surmise donor intent—not an easy task. At times, a board may wonder if they are remaining true to the donor's wishes. If the donor isn't there to ask, how will they know?

Without a donor intent statement, passing on the values to subsequent generations can prove difficult. For example, according to one family foundation trustee, "We had to rely on word of mouth, informal discussions and board retreats to share the donor's interests and intent for the foundation's giving." The foundation urges its colleague foundations to develop an oral history or video, or some other method to guide future generations.

Donors who *do* record their intent and philanthropic vision give future board members a clear understanding of the foundation and its mission. Sure, documenting intent can be a lengthy and expensive project—but it doesn't have to be. There are simple ways to do this: Ask your donor(s) to craft a one- or two-page

---

Peer Practices

Creating a Foundation History

The Nathan Cummings Foundation commissioned a history in the form of a 62-page book—*A Family Foundation: Looking to the Future, Honoring the Past.* "We wanted a vehicle to transmit the founding values and dynamics of the foundation to successive generations, as well as an orientation tool for non-family members and staff," said Treasurer Robert Mayer, Ph.D. "We recognized that so much of the wisdom and insight of those who were present at the beginning would be lost or misinterpreted over the years unless we captured it."

Direct costs included hiring a writer and editor, paying for design and printing, and uploading the booklet to the website. Other investments included the substantial time that both staff and board members made available for interviews with the writer as well as research and production of archived documents from the family and foundation.

"The book continues to be an important element of our orientation process for both family and non-family alike," said Mayer. "As time goes on, it serves as an important reminder of how it all began and those very critical initial values and aspirations which created this enterprise. It will also serve as a continuing inspiration to the many generations that follow, who will never have the benefit of personally knowing those pioneers."

letter or interview them on an audio or video recording. *(See section D of this chapter for more on audio and video interviews.)*

A piece of advice: Don't get bogged down in the method of recording intent. Focus instead on the message itself. Start by asking the donor (or yourself, if *you* are the donor) a few questions:

- Why did you start the foundation?
- Why is charitable giving important to you?
- Should the foundation exist forever? Why or why not?
- What would you hope for the foundation to accomplish in 10, 20, 50 years?
- How important is keeping the family involved?
- What parts of your foundation's mission and grantmaking would you like to see remain constant?
- What aspects of the foundation have the potential to evolve—based on the changing needs of the community and/or the changing interests of the family?

It's important that donors articulate some level of flexibility in their intent. *(See section H for more on flexibility.)* This will help future trustees accommodate a changing world—and a changing family. With some flexibility, future trustees have the opportunity to respect the donors' wishes *and* the freedom to keep the mission relevant to the needs of the community and the passion of the board.

For more information on interviewing, read "The Guide for Interviewing Family Members," Family Advisor Series: Archiving Your Family Foundation, *Council on Foundations. Visit* www.cof.org.

Peer Practices
Trusting Future Generations
When James R. Thorpe died in 1978, he left the stewardship to nephews and nieces, giving them leeway to change the foundation's guidelines over the years to reflect current situations. "I think Jim trusted that the ensuing board would make the right decisions and do it in a fair way," said Edith Thorpe, president. Although the board no longer funds the same organizations as the founder once did, "his values and basic principles are still being carried through today."

B. PRESERVE THE FOUNDATION'S EVOLUTION BY COMPILING BOARD DOCKETS AND GRANTS MADE.

Why preserve board minutes and a list of grants made? Because your successors can refer to these documents in the future and learn from them. New board members who take the time to review board dockets, past grants and donor intent will learn about the foundation's history and where it should go.

Before you purge old and unused files into the trash or recycling bin, consider starting a foundation archive. Archiving may sound intimidating at first, but it actually can be simple and fun. Think of an archive as creating a collection of files which become a time capsule for the future.

Archives include files with detailed information about your foundation's beginnings—its values, mission and grant program—as well as its people—the founder(s), trustees and any staff. By keeping an archive, you preserve your foundation (and family) history, showing how it evolved over time. This can provide an important tool to pass on the foundation's values to future trustees, children and grandchildren.

Not only are archives important for your own family, but also for history books. Archives teach the public about philanthropy from a historical perspective and are an important source for understanding the role of philanthropy in America.

What should an archive contain? Ask yourselves: *What will be important for the foundation's successors to know? What would a philanthropy scholar find interesting?* Here are some ideas:

- Minutes from board meetings
- Grant-related files
- Annual reports
- Oral and/or written histories
- Press clippings
- Photographs
- Videos
- Significant correspondence
- A family tree (as applicable).

If you don't have the space (or interest) in storing an archive yourself, consider donating it to a local library, repository or historical society. Most have tools to preserve your materials and can advise you on what is of historical value. For more information on where to donate your archive, contact the Special Collections and Archives at the Indiana University (email speccoll@iupui.org) or the Society of American Archivists (www.archivists.org).

For a collection of articles and tips on archiving, read the Family Advisor Series: Archiving Your Family Foundation, *Council on Foundations. Visit* www.cof.org.

In Their Own Words

The Importance of Archiving

"Foundations should think through the archiving of minutes, annual reports and other documents to preserve the history in a public fashion for scholars. Foundation activity is very interesting to cultural and intellectual historians of communities, and records should be made available, after a reasonable period of time, to scholars and the general public."

—*Al Castle, executive director, Samuel N. & Mary Castle Foundation*

C. INVITE SENIOR FAMILY MEMBERS TO SPEAK WITH THE BOARD.

Some of the richest moments in the boardroom occur when senior family members tell stories—sharing their lives, their past and their connection with the foundation.

Stories often capture the foundation's history and core values. They allow new trustees to hear—in the voices of founding members—why the foundation started, what choices the family made and how the foundation evolved over time.

Stories not only convey a portrait of another time, but also can reenergize the current board. Think about how you feel when you hear an old story—more connected, somehow, to the people and places the story is about. Listening to older members reminds the board they are part of something larger than themselves—and grounded in something as intimate, and individual, as family.

If you give senior family members time to talk about themselves, they will often reveal why they joined the board and what their underlying philanthropic values are. They will enjoy remembering why they chose to serve on the board—and the younger generation will appreciate learning the background and talents of their family members.

Quick Tip

Ask senior or retired trustees to pick one word from the mission statement and describe what it means to them.

Senior family members bring many perspectives, expertise and interests to the table. Most often, the board might ask them to speak during a new board member orientation. You might also invite them to talk at a board retreat, a holiday gathering or other family event.

Consider including senior members periodically in your board meetings. If time allows, ask them to tell a short story. *How did they become involved in the foundation? What do they like best about serving on the board? What do they remember about the founders?*

Some senior members might feel uncomfortable in the spotlight. Remind them that storytelling doesn't have to be a planned and polished presentation. In fact, the best stories are fluid—those that emerge, unplanned, from a conversation. If the members have an old photo album or a scrapbook to share, ask them to bring it along. Sometimes these items can spark a story in themselves.

"We all have a story to tell about our lives and visions and through our foundations we are inviting others to work with us toward that vision."

—Bill Graustein, trustee,
William Caspar Graustein
Memorial Fund

In Their Own Words

Tales of Legacy

"Since two of our four board members, my mother and my aunt, are first generation trustees in their 70s, we have realized we face generational changes. Several years ago, we gathered our families and children for a retreat. We told stories about our mother and grandmother, Lydia Stokes, about her philanthropy and our own, and about the foundation. Many of our early discussions centered on how to include the next generation. My mother and my aunt each wrote a legacy letter about their mother (our founder) and her philanthropy, including our foundation's philosophy. We sent this letter to my sister and cousin to begin to generate their interest. As for the children in our next generation, we're working to bring them gently into the loop."

—Nancy Deren, trustee, Lydia B. Stokes Foundation

Talks Build Family Relationships

"They will have a series of conversations with members of the family, where the older family members can share their knowledge on various nuts and bolts about the foundation—finance, grantmaking, history and more. This will teach the new members and, at the same time, encourage relationships among the family."

—Julie Simpson, executive director, Cricket Island Foundation

D. Collect personal recollections of the foundation through interviews with the donor(s) and/or senior board members (audio, video and/or written).

Heard one family story, heard them all? Maybe this is true for you, but how can you make sure those foundation stories get passed on to your children and grandchildren—the board members of the future?

Get ready to take your foundation's storytelling to the next level. To preserve your foundation's history, you must *record* it. What better way to do so than in the voice of the donors themselves?

Sounds technical, but it doesn't have to be. All you need is a tape recorder, a video recorder, a pen and paper, or a word processing program. Start by asking the donor to write a letter or brief memoir about his or her life. If the donor isn't a wordsmith, you might hire an outside author to write a family foundation history—which could include photographs and even a family tree.

Other foundations take a different approach by audio- or videotaping an interview with the donor (and/or senior family members). If you go the video route, you can hire a professional videographer or ask a volunteer from the family who knows how to use a camera. Regardless of how you document the foundation's history, be sure the history is tied to the foundation and not merely the family. In most cases, researching the family's geneology, history and stories unrelated to the foundation is not considered a charitable activity and should be conducted and funded by sources other than the foundation.

It helps to prepare questions in advance of the interview. To help you jump-start the conversation, here are some you might consider:

- Why did you start (or join) the foundation?
- What were the key moments in your life that made you think about helping others?
- When was the first time you volunteered your time or talents?
- Who were the major influences in your life, and how did they influence your philanthropy?
- What did you hope to accomplish through a foundation, and has that changed over time?
- What do you consider the foundation's biggest success?
- What is the most important value you hope to pass on to your family?

Here's a tip: Children can be great interviewers. Senior family members may feel more motivated, and even more relaxed, sharing the family's stories with children than with a professional or adult family member. Plus it's a great way to involve the children early in the family's philanthropy.

"Foundation stories develop a lore that can capture the purpose of the foundation in a rich, nontechnical way... keeping past success stories fresh."

—Brooke Lea, trustee, Helen Sperry Lea Foundation

Peer Practices

Foundations on Film

The Halcyon Hill Foundation preserved the values of its founder on videotape. "The founder's storytelling was one we wanted to capture somehow," recalled Director Annette Weld. In a group decision, the family hired a local videographer who developed questions on why the founder started the foundation and how it had changed over the years. The 25-minute video includes the candid responses of the founder and her three adult children, along with archival photos and footage of the children and grandchildren.

"It took several months for planning, logistics and the final production, although the actual filming was completed in a single morning, just before a board meeting," says Weld. "The video itself is simple—no fancy graphics. It may not win any Academy Awards, but we found it made for an intimate setting, where the family members could recall their feelings about the foundation."

The production costs were about $8,000, which included 20 copies made for present and future board members. Although the video is and will be used for foundation purposes, the founder paid for the costs personally.

The video was shown for the first time after a board meeting. According to Weld, "We gathered around with popcorn and Kleenex to watch it for the first time." The video will be used for the family, for new trustee orientation, as well as at retreats. "It's something the kids and grandkids will treasure for generations to come. I feel we should do one every five years."

In Their Own Words

Keeping the Legacy Alive

"Several years ago, my mom said, 'I'm 78. I'm tired. I no longer want to do all the work that goes into grant-making, but I don't want to lose touch with it either.' In order to create an opportunity to keep my mother engaged, we created a new, non-voting trustee position—the Legacy Keeper. This position would allow a trustee to resign from voting and granting, yet remain engaged in the spirit of our activities."

—*Nancy Deren, trustee,*
Lydia B. Stokes Foundation

E. CONDUCT ACTIVITIES THAT PROVIDE SUBSEQUENT GENERATIONS THE OPPORTUNITY TO CONNECT WITH THE FAMILY FOUNDATION HISTORY.

Sometimes you don't even need stories to pass on the history of the foundation—those stories speak for themselves.

For example, some foundations take the younger generation on a tour of the neighborhoods, factory sites or organizations tied to the foundation's history. You might take them to the company or location where the founder made the money that started the foundation. Or take them on site visits—asking your grantees to show them how the foundation's support has made a difference to the people they serve.

Outside of family tours, be sure to include younger generations in family meetings or reunions. The sooner they feel they are a part of the family's philanthropy, the more likely they are to become active in the family's good work.

To share the foundation's values firsthand, introduce the concept of giving to children—early and often. For example, engage them in activities that will spark their interest in charity—family rituals that center around giving or volunteering at a local organization. (*For more ideas on involving children in philanthropy, see chapter 9, section C.*)

In Their Own Words

Growing Up Giving

"While philanthropy was not a word we used in my household while I was growing up, it was a way of life. We never sat down and talked about doing philanthropy; instead, my parents were role models. They were both quite involved in community service and our church. For example, my dad's business made food baskets every Christmas to give to those who needed food that year. Going to the warehouse that Saturday in December was one of the highlights of my holiday. I loved the joy and community spirit that filled the air as we all worked together to compile those wonderful boxes full of food. I loved this day because it embodied the values that were prominent in my house—generosity, honesty, integrity, kindness, compassion, love and gratitude. Although I may not have called it philanthropy, I believed these values were part of my life, and that I needed to live life according to them."

—*Jomie Goerge, trustee, Colina Foundation*

F. Review founding documents and donor intent or preferences periodically to assess their continued efficacy.

Founding documents? Check. Donor intent? Check. Foundation history, interviews and archives? Check, check, check.

Maybe you feel like you're ahead of the game at this point—and you are. But foundation work isn't a one-time job; it's an ongoing process.

You read earlier about the importance of balancing donor intent with changing needs. To keep up this balancing act, your board must periodically review its founding documents and donor intent. As with any organization, there's a danger in running a foundation *status quo*, year after year. Trustees need to be sure that the foundation's mission remains vital and effective.

Take the time to review—and if necessary, redefine—the mission and governance structure of your foundation. Ideally, this should be done once every three to five years.

Below, you will find a sample chart that may help you take a look at your foundation's mission and donor intent in the context of the past, present and future. You might use this as a tool for your board to start the conversation.

Reviewing Our Mission & Purpose	PAST	PRESENT	FUTURE
PROGRAM How we fulfilled our purpose	*We fulfilled our purpose by...*	*We fulfill our purpose by...*	*We will fulfill our purpose by...*
PUBLICS The people we served	*We served...*	*We served...*	*We will serve...*
WHY? The reasons we serve people with our programs	*Because...*	*Because...*	*Because...*

Peer Practices

Revisiting the Donor Intent

As the Clowes Fund found out, it's never too late to review the donor intent. Forty-eight years after its founding, the foundation held a retreat to reevaluate its mission and purpose. "At the retreat there was consensus that family was a core value of the foundation and that to maintain that important core value, it would be necessary for the foundation to have the flexibility to change to reflect the interests of the family as it changes," recalled Executive Director Beth Casselman.

As the children of the third generation took seats on the board, the geographic scope of grantmaking began to expand to reflect the board's interests. Because the family had grown to represent a broad range of interests and geographic locations they considered dividing the fund after the death of the third donor. Instead, the family agreed to respectfully disagree about some issues, such as religion, which was eventually eliminated as an interest area to maintain family harmony.

"Compared with the original donor intent, our mission is now broader in some aspects and more narrow in others," says Casselman. "Although our grantmaking focus has changed since inception, we are confident that the founders would be pleased that the family is still doing good work—together."

Recognizing Later Generations' Interests

G. Encourage board members with interests outside the program guidelines to support them through personal giving.

You know it's important to stick to your foundation's mission over time. But consider this: If your mission is too broad, it could later cause tension among board members, who compete for their own funding interests. And if your mission is too narrow, it might exclude some board members who would rather fund their own favorite causes in their own hometowns.

How do you please everyone, all the time?

Foundation giving isn't a "one size fits all" model. If your board tries to accommodate everyone's outside interests, it will only undercut your program's effectiveness by spreading grants over too wide an area. By no means should the foundation structure *impede* your members' personal giving goals, but remind your board that there are plenty of options for giving—outside the foundation.

Your board should encourage trustees to use their own personal funds to support their own goals—and keep the foundation's giving focused and on mission. Some family branches or individuals establish donor-advised funds through their local community foundations. This allows them to give anonymously or outside their foundation's funding area. Others accomplish the same goals by giving through a public foundation or special interest group that offers donor-advised or similar funds.

Many people would rather keep their personal giving simple through "checkbook giving"—writing checks to their churches, colleges or favorite personal cause.

Recently, giving circles have become a popular giving option. Giving circles (also called *collectives*) offer family foundation members a hands-on giving opportunity—in addition to their foundation giving. A giving circle allows them to pool funds by more than one donor and decide jointly which areas they will fund. *For more on giving circles, read* Family Matters, *Fall 2001, at* www.cof.org.

Peer Practices

Personal Giving Avoids Tension

To avoid potential conflict, the Patrick & Aimee Butler Family Foundation agreed to steer clear of certain controversial issues. For example, the board doesn't fund faith communities or faith-based organizations for religious purposes. It also doesn't fund board members' former colleges and universities. According to Trustee Sandy Butler, "We made an agreement that if you felt strongly about an issue, and it's an issue that would create friction on the board, you should support it yourself personally—without the foundation."

H. IF NOT COUNTER-INDICATED IN THE ESTABLISHING DOCUMENTS, (E.G., TRUSTS) CONSIDER EXPLICITLY ADDING THE FLEXIBILITY TO ADAPT FOCUS AREAS.

Family foundations have an exceptional charge: To honor the founding donor's intent while meeting the community's current needs. As a donor, you can do your future trustees a great service by giving them the flexibility to change the foundation's grantmaking focus. By building in flexibility to the focus areas, trustees will be able to adjust the mission to meet current realities and board interests.

Here are a few ways to accommodate change over time:

- Consider framing your mission statement to reflect short-term and long-term goals. This will allow your larger mission to remain constant, while some aspects of your grantmaking can change.

- Ask younger members of the family (not yet on the board) what they think about your mission and guidelines. You may be surprised at what they say.

- If you haven't done so already, include in your bylaws a description of the process by which they can be changed. That way, trustees will know how to amend the governance structure if need be.

Some donors might not be comfortable with this level of flexibility. After all, it requires you to *trust* that your family members will make the right choices for the good of all. Perhaps they won't be the same choices that you, the donor, would make. If this level of flexibility isn't right for you, you might consider limiting the lifespan of your foundation. (*See chapter 9, section E for information on alternative foundation structures.*)

A word of caution: Sometimes the interests of next generation members compete with older board members—but this healthy tension can lead to good change. Take the Perrin Family Foundation, for example. David Perrin of the Perrin Family Foundation said his parents were pleased that he wanted to serve on the board, but there was some friction over the direction he wanted to take. "Because my mother has been mostly responsible for establishing the foundation, it has been somewhat difficult for her to relinquish control," he said.

When David wanted to allocate funds for a new area of focus, his parents balked. "They said, 'We have no track record in this area and we don't know to whom we're giving it,'" he recalls. David's youthful energy and desire to do things quickly clashed with his parents' more deliberate pace.

As a solution, David received a discretionary grant to fund a youth-activist group, which was located outside the Perrin Family Foundation's traditional geographic funding area. This small step helped the Perrin Family Foundation consider expanding its programming focus to include youth activism and advocacy. As a result, the board redefined its mission to include these new funding areas.

I. If competing interests hinder the foundation's mission or the family's ties, consider engaging a skilled facilitator to find common ground.

In a family foundation setting, misunderstandings, disagreements and power struggles can occur—and in some families, that's considered a good day. As a foundation grows and more people become involved, the level of tension and competing interests can mount. Family members from different branches may share the same blood, but other than that, have little in common.

Here are some common conflicts you might experience on a family foundation board:

- Members of the younger generation have different interests than older members.
- Founders have a hard time passing on control of the foundation to the next generation.
- New family members (such as spouses) do not share the same history or background as the rest of the board.
- Board members persist in their hierarchical family roles—even inside the boardroom.
- Nonfamily members or staff are drawn into unproductive family dynamics.
- Family members hold different interests or religious/political views that affect funding decisions.

Conflict is a natural part of all human relationships and group situations. However, you don't want to let it undermine the effectiveness of your foundation—and take away from the good work you're there to do. Your board will need to distinguish between what is normal, healthy disagreement—and what is simply inappropriate.

In Their Own Words

Helping Consultants Help You

"There are a few things that always help me do my job better as a consultant to a family foundation. One thing a board can do—share with me on a confidential basis information about potentially explosive dynamics that may help avoid some difficult situations and help me develop strategies to keep conflicts from occurring in the future. There is no substitute for complete candor, honesty and full disclosure—all of which are held in confidence."

—*Anne Morgan, consultant*

"We may have debates and discussions at our board meetings, but we end up hugging everybody at the end."

—Charles Huston, III, vice president community relations & director of operations, The Huston Foundation

Because the work is ingrained within a family structure, it requires more participation, commitment and *patience* from everyone involved. Yet, if you find the undercurrent of conflict overruns your board discussion, it may help to hire an outside facilitator for your meetings or retreats.

Facilitators help family members communicate with each other in a way they may not normally be able too in order to get the foundation's work done. The facilitator might be a hired consultant, a family friend or professional associate skilled in facilitation or a colleague from another foundation. The key is finding someone who complements your board's culture and working style.

Boards that use facilitators have said they appreciate having that unbiased person in their midst. The facilitator brings an objective point of view to the table—which can help ensure everyone's voice is heard. For example, the facilitator might keep the conversation on track if it goes astray, prompt non-participators to speak up and, if necessary, diffuse any disagreements or unproductive behavior.

"It's challenging to make sure everyone has an equal voice. We've found it helps to have someone outside the family facilitate," said Amy Zell Ellsworth, board president of the Zell Family Foundation and senior fellow at TPI. The foundation holds one face-to-face meeting per year, and tries to have a facilitator at every one.

Of course, outside facilitators may not be right for every foundation. For some, the outside presence may feel intrusive in the private board or family discussions. "

If your board prefers to keep its decisionmaking on the inside track, consider appointing one of your own to do the facilitating—but beware. Sometimes family dynamics can impede how well someone *within* the family will be able to stay objective in a facilitating role.

When hiring an outside facilitator, what's important is finding the right balance. You can work with individual facilitators to meet your needs. When talking with candidates, consider asking them the following questions:

- How would you work with our foundation?
- What is your facilitation style?
- What other experiences have you had (with other groups, families or foundations) that might help us?
- What fees do you charge? (Ask about fees for preparation time, facilitating the retreat and preparing summary or follow-up reports—facilitators have different ways of billing for time.)

To find facilitators skilled in this area, contact your colleague family foundations, the Council on Foundations or your local regional association of grantmakers for suggestions.

In sum, ask yourselves:

- What does my foundation do to honor and transmit our donor's legacy and the foundation's mission to future generations?

- How do we interpret intent in light of the current needs of our family, community and grantees?

- What steps can I, or my fellow board members, take to incorporate or reconcile differing funding interests?

- What steps can the board take to resolve disagreements?

Resources

Facing Forever: Planning for Change in Family Foundations. By Elaine Gast. Council on Foundations, 2004. Item #847. Visit www.cof.org/publications.

Family Matters newsletters:
- "Death of the Donor" (Fall 2003)
- "Geographic Dispersion" (Summer 2003)
- "The Next Generation Speaks" (Summer 2004)
- "Sharing our Stories" (Fall 2002)

Visit www.cof.org/family.

The Family Advisor: Archiving Your Family Foundation. Council on Foundations. Visit www.cof.org.

The Family Advisor: Generational Succession. Council on Foundations. Visit www.cof.org/family.

The Giving Family: Raising Our Children to Help Others. By Susan Crites Price. Council on Foundations, 2005. Item #822. Visit www.cof.org/publications.

The Succession Workbook: Continuity Planning for Family Foundations. By Kelin Gersick. Council on Foundations, 2000. Item #821. Visit www.cof.org.

A Founders Guide to the Family Foundation: How to Use, Govern and Enjoy Your Family Foundation, Second Edition. Council on Foundations, 2005. Visit www.cof.org/publications.

SAMPLE DOCUMENTS FOR PRINCIPLE VIII

Sample Donor Intent Statement

Courtesy of H.D. (Ike) Leighty, founder of The Leighty Foundation

I have yet to meet a donor or founder of a charitable foundation who said, "When I started out my goal was to make a lot of money so I could give it away."

When I began to realize that I was accumulating more money than I needed, or could reasonably spend, I started to plan to use it to help others. Why? Because of my upbringing—the love, caring and sharing experience from my family, my church and the Christian way of life and what it teaches about service to others, and people like Mother Moon.

I set up the Foundation in 1986 to "park" up to 50% of my income each year while I was deciding where He wanted me to put it to use helping those in need.

My original intent? To do good—whatever that means...

By inviting Bill and Jane, and later Nancy and Bob, to help in finding worthy causes for the funds generated by the Foundation investments, I also visualized it as an opportunity to draw our wide-spread family closer together.

As the Foundation and our roles in it have evolved, we have become aware and sensitive to our diverse interests, which can offer challenges as well as opportunities to us as a family.

My intent has evolved from just "doing good" to the creation of our current mission statement:

"To carry on the Leighty family legacy of service and stewardship by leveraging our time, talents, and finances primarily in the areas of science and the environment, education, spirituality, women's interests, human population, peacemaking, and the promotion of philanthropy and volunteerism."

When we first started, Bill posed the question, "There is so much need out there, why don't we give it all away—put it in the hands of those who can place it where it will do the most good now?"

Good question! I would suggest it be posed and answered at the start of every annual meeting of The Leighty Foundation. We should always be willing to consider a sunset date for the Foundation as an alternative to maintaining it in perpetuity.

I believe the Lord entrusted me with the stewardship of this portion of His great bounty to give me a challenge and opportunity to use it to develop and practice my concern for others—to use me to put His arms around those in need. That has become my intent.

I have invited my family to participate in the stewardship of this challenge and opportunity. Notice that it is not the H.D. Leighty Foundation—it is The Leighty (family) Foundation.

In joining me, the family has received the side benefit of the opportunity to work and draw closer together—and to meet and get to know others who are challenged with similar opportunities—a great group of worthwhile people.

Continued on page 180

It is my intent that we make donations and support causes where our comparatively small amounts of money can be used as leverage—seed money—to attract other givers to the cause or project…the Parable of the Mustard Seed!

It is also my intent that we leverage the time, talent and experience we develop in the members of our family to mentor other potential donors as they discover the joy of giving of their share of His great bounty—to help them establish and grow their own family philanthropy.

I would like us to be "philanthropic missionaries" and regularly allocate a portion of our funds to emphasize and support that part of our mission.

My family is my #1 interest!

I hope that they grow together as stewards of all our family gene pools as well as the Foundation. If at some time in the future, the operation and administration of the Foundation should be in danger of splitting the family apart, it would be my intention that the Foundation and the stewardship of its assets be given to an independent agency such as the Community Foundation of Waterloo and NE Iowa to administer. I have full confidence in my family's ability to choose wisely regarding the health of the family, and the stewardship of the Foundation."

CHAPTER 9
Prepare the Next Generation

PRINCIPLE IX:

WE PLAN FOR FAMILY LEADERSHIP CONTINUITY.

Your family foundation began with certain goals in mind. Without a doubt, those goals will still be important as you think about your foundation's future.

But looking into the future is like peering into the unknown.

Plus, you might feel apprehensive about planning the future of your foundation—a future that, inevitably, one day won't include you.

Still, if you want your foundation to last, planning for leadership continuity is essential. There are many benefits to taking on the issue sooner rather than later. Consider this:

IN THIS CHAPTER

- Develop and implement a succession plan
- Teach young family members about philanthropy
- Periodically revisit the lifespan of the foundation
- Use alternatives when family leadership is no longer viable.

- Planning ahead means being prepared. It's better to talk about succession early, before a crisis makes the discussion necessary.

- Early succession planning will give next generation members plenty of time to learn their leadership roles.

- Senior family members are the best people to pass down the strengths and history of the foundation. It's best to bring on new members while these senior members are still alive and active in the foundation.

- Discussing succession can open doors into other important conversations—for example, the death of the founder, different interests and philosophies among board members, the pressures of geographic dispersal, and more.

Enough to convince you to start planning?

This chapter will take you through the steps to plan for your foundation's leadership well into the future. It might sound complicated—and it is. But with an early start, you'll be able to give your family and foundation time to deal with any challenges that arise. You'll also involve the younger generation in a legacy—something that is up to *them* to continue. With fresh generations of new voices at the table, your family foundation will look forward to new directions, yet to be revealed.

*"We're hoping to involve the fourth generation on the board
in the next five or 10 years…so we've started inviting them to
observe our meetings now."*

—Ron Barnes, executive director, Kenneth T. & Eileen L. Norris Foundation

Practice Options for Principle IX

A. DEVELOP AND IMPLEMENT A SUCCESSION PLAN (WITH INPUT FROM THE FAMILY'S TEENS AND YOUNG ADULTS) TO IDENTIFY, EDUCATE AND PREPARE THE NEXT GENERATION OF FAMILY MEMBERS FOR FUTURE BOARD SERVICE.

It's never too early to prepare the next generation of foundation leaders. But where do you begin?

As with any important decision, you'll want to start with your mission.

What guidance does you mission give regarding succession? Is keeping the family together most important? Maintaining the wishes of the founder? Or something in between?

For example, some families create foundations to keep the family working together over time. That is the foundation's number one goal—above any particular cause or funding area. In other foundations, a social issue or need takes precedence, and it becomes more important to support that cause than to keep the family engaged.

In the words of one family foundation trustee: "Clarify what is most important to your foundation: Is it the family, or is it the mission? That is the well from which you spring." (Nancy Deren, Lydia B. Stokes Foundation)

Once you've examined your mission, there are other important questions to think about as well (some of which have been addressed in *chapter 1*):

- Do you want your foundation to exist in perpetuity?
- If yes, is it a priority for you to see your children take over when you're gone?
- What role do you see the foundation playing in your family?
- What parts of your foundation's mission and grantmaking would you like to see remain constant?
- What aspects of the foundation have the potential to evolve?
- Is there a role for non-family to play?

Once your board has thought about—and more important, discussed—these issues, you are ready to begin your succession planning process.

Simple Steps for Succession Planning

Below are some steps that simplify that process. Be sure to read *The Succession Workbook* (Council on Foundations, 2000) for a more comprehensive outline on succession:

Step One: Your foundation should choose a succession planning leader and/or committee. Someone needs to take the lead in starting—and organizing—the discussion. Who will it be?

Step Two: Decide who will participate in the succession planning process. For example, will you keep the discussion to the current board only? Select representatives from different generations and family branches? Involve all extended family members over 18? Or perhaps offer an open invitation to anyone interested?

Step Three: Conduct a retreat. Retreats can be the best way to get the succession process started and to build enthusiasm among the family. At the retreat, you can gain a shared sense of the importance of succession planning and come up with a tentative plan for the whole process. You might consider hiring a facilitator to guide the retreat.

Step Four: If you haven't done so already, your board should develop eligibility and selection requirements for new board members. This gives you objective guidelines for nominating new members—and for responding to family members who express interest in serving on the board. *See chapter 2 for more information.*

Step Five: Develop a plan for training the next generation. This might include having a series of conversations with older members, inviting the next generation to attend board meetings or site visits, establishing a junior board or matching gifts program and more. Read this chapter for more ideas. Whatever methods you choose, specify a timeframe and success measures for the training period.

With these steps to guide you, let your succession planning begin.

"The younger generation members are really our mentors—and they are quick to tell us what we could be doing better."

—Charles Huston III, *vice president community relations & director of operations, The Huston Foundation*

Just the Facts: Preparing the Younger Generation

According to Council on Foundations research, the most popular way for family foundations to prepare younger family members for board service is through a family retreat. Fully 70 percent chose this option, followed closely by site visits at 65.7 percent. Attending conferences or seminars came in third (45.7 percent), followed by discretionary grants (27.1 percent), matching gifts (22.9), junior boards (22.9) and advisory committees (18.6).

Challenges to Succession

There are a few common challenges when it comes to succession. Learning about them *now* will save you time and headaches later.

As you start your succession planning, you may find your foundation falls into one of two camps. If you're a small family, you might not have many next-generation candidates to choose from (or too few that meet your board's criteria). On the other hand, if you have a large family, perhaps you have the opposite problem—*too many* qualified candidates. Either way, how will you decide?

Some family boards bring on new trustees based solely on their lineage. If they have the right last name, they're on. However, as experienced foundations would agree, it's best to choose board members based on the skills they can bring to the board—not just because they're relatives. You can save your board from a sticky situation by establishing clear eligibility and selection criteria. This will help you bring on the family members who are actually committed to and engaged in the foundation's values and its work.

If you're a small family and are running out of members to take over the foundation work, it might be time to discuss opening up the board to non-family members, or changing the foundation's overall structure (*see section 9 E*).

What if you do have eligible family members, but they don't necessarily want to join? Getting future generations interested in serving on the board can be a challenge. According to a recent Council on Foundations survey, some foundations faced obstacles in developing their board—including next generation members without the time or desire to participate.

Time seems to be a big factor, especially for trustees in their late 20s and 30s. These young people are often starting families of their own and building their careers. They may not have the time to participate in the board's activities, or they may view the foundation as mom and dad's "pet project," not something they feel personally connected to. Moreover, succeeding generations often lack the same level of wealth as the original donor and face money constraints that prevent them from traveling or taking time off work.

As succeeding generations do become involved, beware of increasing tensions on the board. When you add family members from different branches, it can lead to a board composed of people with differing

In Their Own Words

Apprenticeship Programs

"We recently reviewed and changed our policy on family training. Prior to becoming a member of the board, spouses and the third generation were asked to undergo a Foundation Apprenticeship Program, which was a formal training process that lasted two years. As a part of their training, the members trained with me as the executive director, went on site visits and participated in outside training. We created a handbook with important information, including our founding documents.

"Moving forward, this training program won't just be for foundation members only. With a shift in focus to ongoing education, we will expand this program to all family members. What we will change, though, is the formal feel of the program itself. We found we didn't need to be so formal, especially since our family members are already so engaged."

—*Kathleen Fluegel, executive director, HRK Foundation*

values and ideas about philanthropy. This can be creative tension, but if it gets out of hand, your board may need to consider ways of holding unproductive family dynamics at bay.

In spite of all the challenges listed here (and there are no doubt dozens more), succession planning can be one of your board's most rewarding experiences. It can motivate members to strengthen their goals and policies and can bring the family together in ways you never imagined.

Talk to your colleagues and learn what other families have experienced in their own transitions. Take your time and use the models described in this chapter. And as you go forward, remember this: Succession planning is an ongoing process—not an isolated event. When you start thinking about the future, it's only the beginning.

B. INFORM THE BROADER FAMILY OF THE FOUNDATION'S WORK.

Even if your board never includes more than a few members of the family, why not give the extended family the opportunity to learn about the foundation? By including the larger family, you can help them understand the values behind the philanthropy—and possibly gain the interest of younger members.

You might also invite the extended family members to board meetings, family reunions or retreats. At these events, senior board members can speak about the foundation and family history, informing the larger family about what the foundation does. The board might consider inviting one (or more) of its grantees to talk about their organization and a project the foundation supports. Note that expenditure for such events may be reimbursed as educational programs, depending on the structure of the foundation.

Another easy and effective way to keep in touch is through the mail. Try periodically sending a family mailing, such as a quarterly or annual newsletter, or a more personalized family letter. You don't need to print these mailings on expensive paper or have them designed with fancy graphics. You might just write a quick one-pager with the latest news—recent grants, new board members and announcements about upcoming meetings or events. Some foundations send these letters in an electronic (e-mail) format—saving even more time and postage.

One large family that has had success with mailings is the Andrus Family Philanthropy Program, conceived by the Surdna

In Their Own Words

Giving Everyone a Say

"The Cricket Island Foundation is different in that there isn't just one donor who started the foundation. The grandparents suggested that the second generation board members contribute a certain amount. This gave them all joint ownership of the foundation, which has worked well. The foundation was created to involve the family—and given its importance, the board has been struggling with when to allow the third generation to come onto the board and other related questions. For example, the third generation family members (those in their early 20s) are required to make a financial contribution to the foundation before they are eligible to become voting trustees. The family as a whole wrestled with and eventually came to a decision regarding how much each third generation member would be required to give."

—Julie Simpson, executive director, Cricket Island Foundation

Foundation (Andrus spelled backwards). They keep their more than 400 family members informed and involved through an annual newsletter called *Concinnity*, which is the family's special name for its five reunions held since 1973. "The newsletter is an excellent tool for providing awareness, education and, in some cases, opportunities to participate in the family's philanthropic work," said AFPP Executive Director Steve Kelban.

Board and family members write feature stories on the five family philanthropies and short items that highlight a variety of volunteer opportunities. The *Doers* column, in particular, recognizes family members from every generation who have given of themselves and their time. "The stories keep people connected and give them a better picture of each of the family philanthropies." (*To view an issue of Concinnity, visit* www.affund.org/PDFs/ Concinnity.pdf.)

C. PROVIDE AVENUES FOR YOUNGER FAMILY MEMBERS TO LEARN ABOUT AND PARTICIPATE IN THE WORK OF THE FOUNDATION (OR OTHER FOUNDATIONS AND/OR THE NONPROFIT SECTOR) PRIOR TO SERVING ON THE BOARD.

Successful succession begins early, starting with how your family raises its children. To instill the philanthropic spirit at a young age, families should introduce the concept of giving as soon as possible—some say as soon as your child learns to say "mine."

Of course, the best way to teach younger family members about philanthropy is to be good role models yourselves. Yet, there are a number of more proactive ways to get your child involved. Here are some of the most popular:

- Give young children a three-part allowance—divided into money for spending, saving and giving.

- Develop family rituals, such as an annual holiday gift to a needy family or local homeless shelter.

- Volunteer with children in a way that stimulates their interest.

- Establish a matching-gift program, where the child's volunteer services or dollars are matched by a parent, grandparent or other relative.

Consider ways to get young adults involved as well. Even if they aren't yet ready to directly serve on the board, young adults are often eager to participate and will benefit from learning about the family's philanthropy.

Here are some ideas on how your colleagues involve teens and young adults:

- Talk to them about the family history and why the foundation started.

- Take them on site visits, showing them firsthand what the foundation supports.

- Invite them to attend board meetings as observers.

- Encourage them to intern at a local nonprofit organization or a philanthropy program.

- Offer an awards program that recognizes outstanding volunteer work.

- Match a next generation member with a mentor—someone who will show them what it means to be a board member.

- Establish a junior board—where a certain portion of the foundation's grantmaking is set aside for the junior board members to recommend. This can help the next generation understand how money is invested, how grants are made and managed and how the foundation operates.

"Our early foundation involvement brought us [the next generation] together towards a common purpose, using our committee's mission to encompass each member's diverse interest and background."

—Daniel Tarica, Maurice Amado Foundation

In Their Own Words

Next Generation Philanthropy Program

"In 2002, the Lumpkin Family Foundation revisited our strategic plan and decided we needed a way to bring along sixth-generation family members. We established a sixth-generation grants program for kids ages 10 and above. Each member of the Sixth Generation Committee may nominate up to three organizations for a grant. When recommending a grant, members must complete a short application and explain why the organization deserves support. Members will discuss each applicant and agree by consensus or a majority vote whether to make a grant of $100 or $50.

"This has been beneficial by getting the 10- to 14-year-old cousins to work together. That's important because their parents never really got to know each other until into adulthood—and as a result, find it more challenging to work together. Second, it has encouraged the next generation to think about and articulate why some projects are important to them. It has put them into situations where they have to have conversations with their parents about the projects they want to support. Finally, the program—the committee more specifically—has given the staff a good reason to have a relationship with the kids."

—Bruce Karmazin, executive director, The Lumpkin Family Foundation

- Take next generation members to philanthropy conferences and workshops.
- Establish non-voting associate positions, so that they might attend some board and committee meetings

Some advice from next generation family members: Remember to listen to them and respect their input. Nothing will turn them off faster than if they feel you are patronizing them because of their age. Recognize that there is much to be learned from them. Ask them questions and encourage them to offer ideas. For example, if young adult relatives have expertise relating to a particular grant applicant, seek out their advice. Explain why you are considering the applicant in the first place and discuss how this grant fits into your foundation's larger program of giving.

If you include younger members in board meetings or on site visits, ask them later if they understood everything. Reassure them that you, too, had questions when you came onto the board. Give them the comfort level to offer their opinion and the power to implement some of their good ideas.

D. REVISIT PERIODICALLY THE INTENDED LIFE SPAN OF THE FOUNDATION (PERPETUAL OR TIME-LIMITED).

You've no doubt heard the "P" word before. Perpetuity is when a foundation plans to exist, well, forever. Most founders start their foundations with perpetuity in mind, giving their families an entity through which they can work together over time—across generations, in spite of distance and differing views.

But picture yourself four generations and ten family branches later—in a room full of people with different philosophies, values and personalities. Is perpetuity really *practical*, after all?

Even if it's not something you'll decide today, it's worth asking the question. As one philanthropist said, "Perpetuity is a long, long time." How long is *too* long for your foundation?

When it comes to perpetuity, family foundations across the board remain optimistic. In a recent COF survey, 83 percent of respondents said they expect their foundation to exist in perpetuity. Still, many foundations that are established in perpetuity later decide, for any number of reasons, to close their doors. Perhaps there is no next generation of board members to take over. Or maybe the family has grown too large to maintain unity in its interests and ideologies.

Other foundations may consider changing the foundation's lifespan, but then decide they want to stick it out after all. They may redefine the mission to one that's more viable and relevant to the current needs and family interests. Or they might use other tools (a discretionary grants program, for example) in their grantmaking or governance structure to keep the family engaged.

Let's take a look at what some of your colleagues call the "great perpetuity debate."

Those in favor of **perpetuity** say it:

- Creates a lasting legacy where the founder will be remembered by the family and by the public.
- Passes along philanthropic values to future generations.
- Keeps the extended family together over time.
- Creates impact over the longterm, leaving money available for tomorrow's problems.
- As endowment grows over time, it yields more support for grantees.

- Keeps funds available in times of economic downturn—today's surplus can be used for tomorrow's unforeseen needs.

On the flip side, those in favor of a **limited lifespan** say it:

- Allows the donor to see the full effects of the giving in his or her lifetime.

- Recognizes that future generations may fund things the donor would not like.

- Does not bind future generations to an enterprise that may not interest them, takes significant commitment and/or may cause future differences and conflict.

- Creates larger impact in the short-term, making a bigger difference on today's problems.

- Avoids the administrative costs and labor of running a foundation over time.

- Avoids the possibility that the foundation becomes fragmented, ineffective or irrelevant over time.

Both sides make a good case, and it's up to your board to decide which is right for you at any given time. Discuss your foundation's lifespan periodically—at least once every five years—and in times of major change, such as the death of a donor or when bringing on a new generation.

Here are a few questions that will help you start the discussion:

- Is our mission still relevant? Will it be in five, 10, even 50 years?

- What matters more—keeping the family interested or keeping our current program focus?

- Do we believe it's necessary to operate in perpetuity in order to have a long-lasting impact? Could we achieve more impact through concentrated spending now?

- Do we have a pool of next generation people who are interested in participating?

Peer Practices

Spend It Now

When Claude Rosenberg and his wife set up the Louise and Claude Rosenberg Foundation, they chose the standard perpetual structure. Now, said Rosenberg, he and his wife definitely plan to spend down the foundation themselves—"the sooner, the better," he said. "We both feel limited as to how you can control things after you're gone. We very much feel we should do the most we can while we're alive." One reason, he added, is that "the best things we've done have had a little bravery to them. The next generation might be more cautious, since they are using someone else's money. They might feel like they can't stick their necks out as much." While he would like the grandchildren to know the couple is philanthropic, he said "the choice we have is to leave more to the children and have them inherit a broken society or to leave them less money and inherit a better society in which to live their lives."

Excerpt from Facing Forever: Planning for Change in Family Foundations, *Council on Foundations, 2004.*

- Would it be desirable to "sunset"—to close down after a fixed period of years or after the last child or grandchild dies?
- Would family members be upset if the foundation didn't exist in 15 years?
- Would you be upset if the foundation changed its mission?

Closing a foundation, especially where the termination was not envisioned by the donor, can be a complicated legal undertaking. It requires the advice of knowledgeable legal counsel.

In Their Own Words

Keeping the Mission Fresh

"Several years ago, our four trustees nearly disbanded the foundation. We began a retreat at 8:00 a.m. thinking the whole thing was to be dissolved. By noon, with the help of a wonderful facilitator, we were so excited about our mission that it gave us a fresh start. What changed for us in that short time? We decided our foundation is OF the family, not THE family. This was huge for us. We decided our common bond is not because we are family members alone, but because we want to honor the mission and hold true to the founder's legacy and our shared philosophy. Now we want to include our children, address board diversity and plan how to keep the mission fresh as we go forward."

—*Nancy Deren, trustee, Lydia B. Stokes Foundation*

E. EMPLOY ALTERNATIVE GOVERNANCE STRUCTURES OR GIVING VEHICLES WHEN FAMILY LEADERSHIP IS NO LONGER VIABLE OR NO LONGER DESIRED.

The farther away from the founder a family foundation gets, the more likely it is for the foundation to ask a critical question: Should we continue? Faced with a lack of interest or commitment by future generations, or burdened by disagreements among board members, some family foundations eventually decide to call it quits.

Don't feel bad: If your foundation decides to close, it doesn't mean you've failed. It's simply how your board has responded to change, in the best way for everyone involved.

If your family decides that it can no longer manage the foundation, you can consider a number of options: spending down, splitting the foundation or choosing some other alternative structure (such as a donor-advised fund at a community foundation).

Let's look at some of these options and more:

1. **Becoming an independent foundation.** Some family foundations become independent because the founder has no descendents or other close relatives and bequeaths the foundation's leadership to non-family members who are carefully selected for their experience and knowledge and interest. In general, the larger the corpus, the more likely a foundation will evolve into an independent foundation, with little or no family involvement. Though family may no longer wish to be involved, the endowment may be too large to spend out or fold into another entity.

2. **Merging with another foundation.** Merging assets and interests with another foundation may be the best way to preserve a foundation over time. Foundations may merge for a variety of reasons. Some-times merging is out of necessity—there's simply no one to take over the foundation's operations. Others might want to create a stronger, larger entity with more assets or to maximize efficiency by sharing staff, space and resources. There are complex legal rules governing foundation mergers, and foundations should always consult with an attorney before entering into any contract.

3. **Splitting the foundation.** Splitting means closing one family foundation by creating a number of smaller private foundations. In these cases, family branches, generations or other groups take portions of the foundation assets to endow their own separate foundations, with their own grantmaking interests.

   Splitting is an option most common in families with different branches or of varying philosophies. By splitting, family members can carry out the foundation legacy in a way that suits their individual interests and styles.

4. **Transferring to a community foundation or other public charity**. Turning assets over to a community foundation or other public charity is by far the easiest method of terminating a foundation. The private foundation simply distributes its assets to one or more qualifying public charities that have been in existence for at least five years before the transfer date.

   When transferring to a community foundation, family members may specify in advance that their gift be used only for specific purposes or for the benefit of a specific charity. This makes funds available as a permanent asset in a specific community, with the option to direct funds beyond the community. It takes the administrative burden off the family foundation as well—offering a cost-efficient way to manage investments and grantmaking. It's a way for families to stay involved and continue the family's legacy by creating a fund named for the donor or the foundation. To find your local community foundation, visit www.cflocate.org.

   Most other public charities are also eligible to receive your distributions. However, there are some exceptions and specific legal rules are involved. Be sure to check with a knowledgeable attorney.

Peer Practices

One Family Foundation Parts Ways

The Kerr family was separated by geography and interests. Family members debated whether or not to keep the $80 million Oklahoma foun-dation as one endowment with four distinct funding areas or to divide it into separate entities. In the end, the family opted to divide it into four separate foundations.

According to Breene Kerr, chair of the Grayce B. Kerr Fund in Easton, Maryland, "Legally it was more difficult to separate into four founda-tions, and we did lose some econo-my of scale by having smaller endowments. However, in the long run it is easier for each branch of the family to manage a separate founda-tion." Kerr believes that the more people involved in decisionmaking, the less focused these decisions are. Splitting the foundation has allowed the trustees to focus on grantmaking and spend less time on policy decisions. It has also provided opportunities for more family members to participate.

Excerpt from Facing Forever: Planning for Change in Family Foundations, *Council on Foundations, 2004.*

---

5. **Becoming a supporting organization.** Although a family foundation could terminate into almost any type of public charity, one common approach is to terminate and become a supporting organization. A supporting organization is one that achieves its status as a public charity by operating to benefit one or more other public charities.

   When the family foundation becomes a "supporting organization" to a nonprofit or public charity (including community foundations) it continues to exist as a separate 501(c)(3) entity but may choose to relinquish some or all administrative responsibilities. The nonprofit organization appoints more than 50 percent of the board to the family foundation, which then controls all foundation functions.

   Termination under this provision takes a minimum of five years, and specific laws apply. Be sure to check with your attorney, and refer to the Council on Foundation's book, *Facing Forever: Planning for Change in Family Foundations*, available at www.cof.org.

6. **Spending down.** Foundations may derive a great deal of gratification from spending down the total assets of a family foundation. Board members select one or more nonprofit organizations to receive the corpus directly either as a donation to operations or to grow an endowment. When the foundation chooses this option, it will file appropriate dissolution documents with state and federal authorities, grant all of its assets and cease to exist.

   Spending down commits a foundation's assets to current priorities—using resources to address today's problems. The family can still derive the rewards of giving while alleviating the family's responsibility for running the foundation.

After weighing all their options for terminating, some foundation boards may decide to remain the same unified foundation they always were. They all say that they were better off, however, for having had the discussion.

Whatever your foundation decides, remember this: Changing the structure of a private foundation is not a do-it-yourself project. Family foundations considering any of the above options should seek the assistance of expert legal counsel. For more information, read the Council on Foundation's *Facing Forever: Planning for Change in Family Foundations*, available at www.cof.org.

In Their Own Words

Spending Down? Tell Grantees in Advance

"I'm a great believer if you've funded an organization for a long time, you don't have to fund it forever. Someone else will step up to fund it; the organization will get along without you. But you don't want to take everything away from them in one fell swoop. I told grantees that I was spending down and made a small parting gift to them (a portion of the grant money they had been receiving). There has been no hostility or disappointment expressed on the part of the grantees for the decision I made."

—Raquel Newman, The CM/Raquel H. Newman Charitable Trust

Excerpt from Facing Forever: Planning for Change in Family Foundations, *Council on Foundations, 2004.*

In sum, ask yourselves:

- Is perpetuity right for us? Why or why not?

- Do we have a succession plan that serves the foundation's current leadership, while also engaging younger family members?

- How do we reach out to the extended family, informing them of the foundation's work?

- What do we do to teach young family members about the foundation and philanthropy in general?

- What would the foundation do in the event of the unexpected death or departure of the donor or other board members?

- Has the foundation considered alternative structures if perpetuity is no longer realistic?

Resources

Closing a Foundation: The Lucille P. Markey Charitable Trust. By John Dickason and Duncan Neuhauser. Council on Foundations, 2000. Visit www.cof.org/publications.

Connecting to Your Family Foundations: A Primer for the Next Generation. By the National Center for Family Philanthropy. Association of Small Foundations, 2005. Visit www.smallfoundations.org.

Facing Forever: Planning for Change in Family Foundations. By Elaine Gast. Council on Foundations, 2004. Item #847. Visit www.cof.org.

The Family Advisor: Generational Succession. Council on Foundations. Visit www.cof.org.

"Forever is a Long Time," *Foundation News & Commentary*, July/August 2003. Council members can access the full article at www.foundationnews.org.

The Giving Family: Raising Our Children to Help Others. By Susan Price. Council on Foundations, 2005. Item #822. Visit www.cof.org/publications.

Making Plans for Succession: What Founders Need to Know. By the National Center for Family Philanthropy for the Association of Small Foundations, 2005. Visit www.smallfoundations.org.

Splendid Legacy: The Guide to Creating Your Family Foundation. National Center for Family Philanthropy, 2002. Visit www.ncfp.org.

The Succession Workbook: Continuity Planning for Family Foundations. By Kelin Gersick. Council on Foundations, 2000. Item #821. Visit www.cof.org.

Websites

Resource Generation—Resource Generation works with young people with financial wealth who are supporting and challenging each other to effect progressive social change through the creative, responsible and strategic use of financial and other resources. Visit www.resourcegeneration.org.

21/64—21/64 offers a set of philanthropic tools, networks and communication methods to assist families during these times of generational transition. Visit www.2164.net.

Sample Succession Policy Draft

Courtesy of the Lydia B. Stokes Foundation, DRAFT 8/5

I.   Create an advisory trustee position/role titled Legacy Trustee

II. Develop plan of how to deal with illness/accident/leave of absence on the part of individual trustees

III. Develop process to identify, interview, and retain new Board members

1. Advisory or Legacy Trustee (LT) Legacy Keeper

Trustee resigns as voting member and accepts appointment to non-voting position. Remaining board determines to appoint that member to the non-voting position of Legacy Trustee.

The Legacy Trustee Position:

Non-voting position

Attend meetings and conference calls

Teach/orient new trustees

Give viewpoints, reminder of Legacy, expertise

Legacy Keeper:

 Records and relates stories of family and foundation

 Transfer of intention, principles of foundation

 Instruct new Board members

2. Process to identify and engage new Board Members

Start with family

The foundation is OF the family, not THE family.

Philosophy, principles and intention are the foundation from which we operate:

 Consensus

 Respect

 Spirit

 Legacy

 Connection

 Philosophy

The familial connection is what makes this unique.

3. List potential candidates:

1. Family members-direct line, cousins

2. Spouses

3. Long time friends

4. Philanthropic contacts

4. Addition Process

1. Trustee gives one year notice of desire to leave Board, except in case of illness or emergency.

2. Trustees decide on list of 2-3 potential candidates.

3. Interview process begins. (See below).

4. Trustees have telephone meeting about potential candidate, if candidate is interested in joining, and come to consensus to ask candidate to join board.

5. Trustee who interviewed the candidate invites them to join the board.

6. Candidate has 60 days to decide.

7. Current Trustees sign Determination letter, adding new Trustee to Board.

8. Candidate becomes Trustee at next annual meeting. Pratt video and Q&A evening is held. Legacy Trustee in charge of setting up video, stories, Q&A.

9. New Trustee attends COF Institute for new board members and/or COF annual family foundation conference during first year.

5. Interview Process

1. *One or two current trustees meet with potential candidate to assess potential.*

2. *Report to board.*

3. If potential candidate seems promising, hold another meeting to introduce the idea of joining the board. Give our info (mission statement, guidelines, investment policy, list of grants) for them to take home and ponder.

4. If positive, two current trustees interview the candidate within 30 days.
   Candidate has 60 days to decide and let us know.

   > Legacy trustee(s) would begin new member orientation and mentoring including attending COF family foundation conference
   >
   > New trustee would be welcomed and formally join board at next annual meeting. Term would begin at that point.

6. Term limits

Original family members exempt. Applies to board members added after 2004.
Provide safety valve for board and for each member. Initial two-year term for new trustees. Subsequent, renewable three-year terms, <u>or</u> subsequent renewable five-year terms. Beginning date is July at annual meeting. If Board has a consensus to not retain a member after three-year term, that member must resign.

Continued on page 196

INITIAL TWO YEAR TERM

Year One

Term begins at annual meeting.

Transition ceremony.

Show Pratt video, stories of Legacy and family, Q&A during annual meeting.

First Fall:

New Trustee:

Is included in fall conference call.

Fall grants to be sent ahead of time to new Trustee.

Attends COF Institute for new board members, RAG or COF family foundation conference during the first year.

First Spring

New Trustee:

Works with other Trustees to make grants.

Goal of first year is for new Trustee to get an understanding and feel for the Foundation.

What makes the LBS Foundation unique? What are we all about?

Year Two

New Trustee begins own grant making

Interview Questions:

- What has been important to you in your life?
- What are your most important life values/principles?
- What organizations have you supported with donations, and/or time?
- What causes are important to you?
- What principles are important to you in your business life? How do you conduct your business life?
- How are you involved in your community?
- How do you participate in charitable giving?
- What gifts/talents can you bring to this foundation?
- Do you see yourself having adequate time for this work? (e.g., two conf calls, annual meeting, site visits, researching grantees, COF and RAG education)
- Would you be interested in spending time finding out about organizations in your area to support? Would you be willing to do site visits and follow ups?
- Would you be able to attend the annual meeting each year?
- How do you feel about joining a board that has been small and very close in its sense of family, and commitment to principles?
- How do you feel about being part of an extended family group?
- Have you had much experience with, or have you been interested in, philanthropic activities? If so, what are they?

- What does philanthropy mean to you?
- What is your philosophy regarding socially responsible investing? Do you utilize guidelines in your own investment choices?
- Are you acquainted with Quaker philosophy and peace work?
- Do you have any questions regarding our mission statement? Do you agree with its philosophy?

Orientation/Mentoring Process:

V. Family and foundation history.

VI. Legal requirements of the foundation.

VII. Administration and organizational structure.

VIII. Areas of giving and specific grants.

New trustee gets packet containing:

- Mission statement
- Grantee guidelines
- List of grants for past 3 years
- Investment policy SRI guidelines
- Copy of chapter in Legacy book
- Pratt video-show at annual meeting
- Stories/transcripts of Grandmother and family
- Legal aspects of foundations and trustee responsibilities
- COF standards of practice
- Materials on grant writing
- Pertinent publications, books

Sample Associates Program

Courtesy of the Emily Hall Tremaine Foundation, Inc.

Associate Pool

All family members' aged 16–70 are considered Associates of the Foundation. The Associates Program current priority is the third generation.

In addition, the Foundation encourages families with children under 16 to actively nurture their children's sense of philanthropy and civic participation in their respective personal contexts.

Goal

The Program seeks to build family unity while inspiring the next generation of the Tremaine family to be interested and qualified to join the Foundation Board. The Program's activities allow the Associates to become thoughtful and enthusiastic contributors to the Foundation's development.

Objective

To provide third generation associates with opportunities for training and skill development towards becoming qualified Board members.

Standards for Associate Director Election

Candidates for election as Foundation Associate Directors must demonstrate that they have the requisite

- time,
- interest,
- commitment to family values (as articulated in the Founding Principles), and
- commitment to philanthropy.

As it elects Associate Directors from the G3 pool, the Board will be assessing candidates against the core qualifications and key attributes listed in the Core Document book. The Board will use such indicators as a candidate's level of engagement in the Foundation and its G3 programs, work in the community, other Boards on which the candidate serves, background and training.

Once elected, the Board will support Associate Directors in developing their broader understanding of the philanthropic community through attendance at educational/conference activities sponsored by the Council of Foundations.

Prerequisites

Within three years prior to the proposed Associate Director election date, the candidate **must**:

- have served at least one term on a Foundation Program Implementation Committee; Investment or Associates Committee;
- have been briefed by a Foundation staff member on the Foundation's operations and management systems.

Programmatic Elements

Committees

The Associates Program is centered on Program Implementation Committees, or Investment Committee service as the primary vehicle for Director training.

Associates Grant-making Group (AGG)

As an extension to the cooperative strategy development exercises implemented from 1997-1999, and building on the lessons learned from subsequent experiences, the Board will create a pooled grant-making opportunity which leaves greater initiative with the G3s. The opportunity is only available to Associates under the age of 35, and the goal is to encourage them to work cooperatively, gain insight on co-creative grant development, and develop experience in evaluating grants including budget, program impact and strategy.

The Board will allocate up to $35,000 from the grant distribution budget every year to be awarded by the AGG. Recommendations for allocation of these funds must be presented to the Associate Committee for official approval. The Associates are allocated staff support in developing their program focus area as well as the individual grants.

Matching Grant Opportunity

The Foundation will continue to provide G3s with the opportunity to make personal contributions to local, community-based organizations. These donations will be matched by the Foundation along the guidelines and requirements specified in the Matching Grant Program description.

Retreat

The Foundation will hold an Associates meeting annually. The meeting provides a forum to:
- build family unity,
- enhance skills for group decision-making,
- assess Foundation alignment with family values and vision, and
- brief the entire family on the Foundation's strategic direction.

APPENDIX
Services for Family Foundations

ENRICH YOUR FAMILY'S PHILANTHROPY

As family foundations evolve, they are faced with many questions: What are our giving options? Who should we include on the board? How should we manage the foundation? How do we prepare for generational succession?

The Council on Foundations helps families find answers to these questions and more. The Council's Family Foundation Services (FFS) department provides resources and tools to help family foundations develop and strengthen their philanthropy. Services include technical assistance, professional development, peer connections, publications, leadership opportunities and our premier annual event—the Family Foundation Conference. Through these and other Council services, donors, trustees, family members and staff alike can enhance their knowledge and skills and become more effective grantmakers.

What the Council Can Do for You

Individualized Assistance

- FFS offers you one-to-one assistance on questions about family dynamics, governance,management and grantmaking. We maintain a clearinghouse on family philanthropy—an extensive collection of articles, sample policies, grant guidelines, positiondescriptions and other resources you need to run your family foundation well.

Professional Development

The Council sponsors a variety of educational programs for the beginner and experienced, board member or staff, including:

- Family Foundation Conference, the only national gathering for family foundations
- Next Generation Retreat, for new and soon-to-be board members
- Symposium for Experienced Grantmakers, for foundation leaders with several years of experience in the field

Skill-Building

The Council offers skill-building resources on:

- Foundation governance, management and grantmaking
- Generational succession
- Trustee responsibilities
- Family foundations and the law
- Trends in family foundations
- Media relations
- Philanthropic values in children
- Venture philanthropy
- And more.

Peer Connections and Leadership Opportunities

The Council provides peer-to-peer networking opportunities to broaden your connections with other family foundation donors, trustees and staff. You can also share knowledge, skills and lessons learned with other grantmakers at Council conferences or by participating on one of our committees or e-mail lists.

Publications

The Council is your primary source for critical resources in the field.

Family Matters is a quarterly e-newsletter covering one issue in depth. *Family Matters Now* is a monthly e-newsletter with information from the Council, affinity groups, regional associations and other colleagues. Board Briefings issue papers present both sides of a topic for board discussion and policy formulation. The Council also publishes many books to assist family foundations in all aspects of foundation operations. See our publications catalog or visit www.cof.org for a complete list. Popular titles include:

- *Family Foundations and the Law: What You Need to Know,* Third Edition
- Family Foundation Library Series
- *The Guide to Small Foundation Management—From Groundwork to Grantmaking*
- *The Succession Workbook—Continuity Planning for Family Foundations*
- *The Giving Family: Raising Our Children to Help Others*
- *Facing Forever: Planning for Change in Family Foundations*
- *Grantmaking Basics I* and *II*
- *A Founder's Guide to the Family Foundation*

Legal and Media Services

The Council offers legal information and media consultation, guiding you on IRS legal requirements (e.g.. payout, self-dealing), director's and officer's liability insurance, conflicts of interest and media communication.

Collaboration and Partnerships

The Council works in partnership with the Forum of Regional Associations of Grantmakers (The Forum), which represents 31 of the largest regional associations (city, state or multistate) in the United States, and numerous affinity groups, which represent funding interests (e.g., education, arts) and population groups. Many family foundations join the Council and participate in their regional association and selected affinity groups. (For more information on The Forum, visit www.givingforum.org, e-mail info@givingforum.org or call 202/467-1120. For general affinity group information call 202/467-0382.)

Get to Know the Family Foundation Services Staff

Managing Director Susan Price
202/467-0436, price@cof.org

Information Coordinator Larry Foxman
202/467-0407, foxml@cof.org

Operations Coordinator Christina Dokken
202/467-0476, dokkc@cof.org

Vice President for Constituency Services Char Mollison
202/467-0381, mollc@cof.org.

INDEX